Rays of Hope

Rays of Hope

Poems of Faith and Inspiration

Karyl J. Leslie

Copyright © 2014 by Karyl J. Leslie.

Library of Congress Control Number: 2014917862
ISBN: Hardcover   978-1-4990-8042-1
              Softcover   978-1-4990-8044-5
              eBook   978-1-4990-8043-8

All rights reserved. No part of this book may be reproduced or transmitted in any form or by any means, electronic or mechanical, including photocopying, recording, or by any information storage and retrieval system, without permission in writing from the copyright owner.

This book was printed in the United States of America.

Rev. date: 10/08/2014

To order additional copies of this book, contact:
Xlibris LLC
1-888-795-4274
www.Xlibris.com
Orders@Xlibris.com
686745

Contents

Introduction

Rays of Hope 13

January Readings

Blessing for the New Year 17
Prayer for a New Year 19
I Hereby Resolve… 21
Adding Prayer 23
The Epiphany Star 25
Epiphany (January 6) 26
Light in Darkness 28
Angels – Messengers of God 29
Snow Bird 30
Seasons 31
An Order for Worship 32
In the Beginning 33
Snowstorm 34
Ordained 35

February Readings

God's Love A-Z 39
Winter 40
A Fact of Life 41
Happy Valentine's Day 42
To My Friend… 43

Wonderful Worship..44
A Lovely Time of Worship...46
Brand New Day...47
God Be With You..48
A Teddy Bear Song...49
Ash Wednesday...51
Retirement..54

March Readings

Glory..57
Lenten Theme...58
A Truth..61
On Suffering..62
In Whose Eyes?...64
Kite-Flying..65
Joining In..66
Stormy Weather..67
Guidance...69
Smile..71
"What Can Separate Us…?"..72
Springtime's Best...74
Rainstorm...76

April Readings

Palm Sunday...79
Holy Week: Monday..80
Holy Week: Tuesday..81
Mandatum (Maundy/Holy Thursday).................................82
Why Do They Call It Good?..86
Comparatively Speaking (Good Friday).............................89
Good Friday Poem..91
The Waiting Game (Holy Saturday).....................................97

Easter Greeting 99
Christ Lives! 100
Easter Monday 102
New Life 103

May Readings

Thank You, God 107
My Artist Friend 108
Colors of Life 109
Height 112
A Gracious Nod 113
Hearty Belief 114
Never Too Old 115
Sacred Rest 118
Peace to You 119
Bird Song 120
Truly Blessed 121
Retreat 124

June Readings

An Important Invitation 127
Pentecost Day 129
Summer with God 130
Any Sunday Morning 132
A Timid Old Man 137
Simple Prayer 138
On Arising 139
Patience 140
My Prayer 141
Where Has the Lord Gone? 142
Breezes 143
A Parting Prayer 144

July Readings

It's About Time	149
Hope	152
Ready for the Day	153
Good Morning, Good Day	154
New Eyes	156
And the Lord…	157
The Holy One	159
Time to Dream	161
Singing Praise	162
Blue Sky	163
Psalm 19, rephrased	164
Trusting God in Difficult Times	165
Poetry	168
Condolences, Part 1	169
Condolences, Part 2	172

August Readings

Answered Prayer	177
Patterns of Prayer	178
God Is Good	179
Sweet Slumber	181
Choices	182
Blessings	183
Your Story	186
New Beginnings	187
Joyful Kindness ABC	190
A Better Chance ABC	191
The Open Door ABC	192
Dedication	193
Nighttime Rest	194
An Important Lesson	195

September Readings

Changes 199
Everyone, Back to School! 200
Sunday Morning 203
Your Part 204
May Your Skies Be Blue 207
A Long, Long Day 208
Gifts to One Another 209
Today's Blessing 211
Simple Relief 212
A New Song 213
Peace 214
Humble Prayer 215
Miraculous Day 216

October Readings

Party Time 219
Holy Communion 220
Autumn Changes 223
Autumn Blessings 224
Autumn Speaks 227
October Extravagance 228
Comfort 230
Daily Prayer 231
Peaceful 232
A New Stage of Life 233
Live in Hope; Build on Dreams 236
Indescribable 237

November Readings

A Morning Prayer 241
In Perfect Harmony? 242

The Spice of Life	244
If You Are Lonely	246
Delighted?	247
Precious Variety	249
It Hurts to Keep It Inside	250
A Song of Gladness	252
Benediction	253
I Need You, Lord	254
Trees	255
Every Day Thanksgiving	257
Let Us Thank Our God Above	258
Evening Song	260

December Readings

Advent Blessings	263
Preparing the Way	265
Secrets	267
"In the Beginning Was the Word"	268
Christmas Again	270
A Christmas Blessing	273
Christmas Eve	274
My Christmas Prayer for You	278
Sparkling, Holy Light	279
Immanuel – God Is With Us	280
New Year's Eve	282

Introduction

We all need hope. The purpose of this book is to provide rays of hope through the use of poetry. This book can be used either as an occasional devotional resource or can be read at will. It is intended to inspire readers toward a healthy, healing, and hopeful faith in God; to help them see and believe in possibilities, miracles, and their own dreams and potentials; to inspire them to reach out to others with their own gifts. It's intended to nurture hope for this life, but not for this life only. Ideally readers will be inspired to reach out to and maybe inspire others with their own hopeful thinking and hopeful living.

The poems in this volume point regularly to the love, promises, and faithfulness of God. The reader is encouraged to use the open space on each page for his or her own reflections, expressions, or prayer. The variable length and style of the poems is deliberate to enable a variety of reflection experiences and opportunities.

Thank you to Carissa Simon of Carissa Simon Photography for the author photo on the back cover.

Rays of Hope

"Rays of Hope" it's titled,
And it is designed
To be a book of poems
That can cheer the mind.

The notion is quite simple:
That this will be a book
That can help to build faith
For those who choose to look.

Its style is quite poetic.
It can be read each day
With space on every page
For what you'd like to say.

You could write your own thoughts
And your own prayers as well
In the empty spaces
When you stop and sit a spell;

For in every sitting,
Some hope can be found
If you give to yourself
The chance to look around.

God cannot be taken
Out of life, you see,
For everywhere that you are,
God is sure to be.

January Readings

Blessing for the New Year

May blessings come upon you
In the year that will unfold
Before you in this new year,
Blessings all untold.

May God be with you every day,
And may you seek God's will,
For God's will is what's best for you.
I pray you know that still.

May blessings all abundant
And deep and rich and true,
And those beyond what you might hope,
Come true for you and you.

I pray you know God's love is
There for you every day,
And God knows each and every prayer
Before you can even say

What it is that you desire,
What you hope will be,
How you want to thank your God
With gratitude so free.

I pray for you a story
That unfolds in chapters new
That can turn around your life
As God's will you seek to do.

May God's blessings be upon you
As you enter this new year,
And may you know the greatest gift
Of the Savior's grace so dear.

Turn your life around this year
In whatever way you need,
And dedicate to holy God
Your every waking deed.

Prayer for a New Year

It is now a brand new year.
May we have a vision clear
That we may see the goals we might
Achieve in keeping holy sight.

The path God sets lies just ahead.
God keeps our hearts and spirits fed
With God's own Word if we rely
On God's strength and don't just try

To make our way all on our own.
We never have to be alone,
Because our God is always there
And answers every hidden prayer.

The answer may be "Yes" or "No,"
Or even "Wait" may be the tone
Of what God says to our requests.
We mustn't make our prayers a test

To see if God loves us enough
To give whatever we ask of
God when we take time to pray.
God's answer is sometimes, "Just wait,

And you will see amazing things,
And maybe even angels' wings.
I love you and will hold you fast."
What more could we really ask

But to be held in God's strong grip
Whether we go out on a trip
Or just stay home and do our work.
God's love is what makes our hearts perk

Like the coffee we heat up
And pour into a waiting cup
To give us warmth and some caffeine
Or maybe just some lovely steam.

Hold out your cup for God to pour
Treasures into it once more;
And may you come once more to know
God's blessings truly overflow.

I Hereby Resolve…

New Year's resolutions, they say,
Are good to make each New Year's Day,
But, "Bah! Humbug!" is what you say?
You can't keep yours for a single day?

Look ahead for some good advice
About how to make next New Year nice –
Or maybe there's still help this year.
Maybe things will become quite clear

As you read some suggestions fine
About how you can redeem the time.
Don't set yourself up to fail again.
This works for me. You try it then.

Don't resolve to do one hundred percent
Whatever it is that's your intent.
Perfection, you know, is nearly nil
For those of us on this planet still.

So set yourself some reasonable goals.
Be sure you can do them, not dig a hole.
Aim to do such-and-so three days a week.
All seven days is too much to seek.

You want to change your life somehow?
You want to do it starting now,
But seven days a week you don't think you can
Stick to your promise, keep to your plan?

Then promise yourself that you will try
For three days a week. I think that'll fly.
Sure, aim for seven, but don't beat your head
If up to four of those days have sped

By you that week without having been
Noted for what you'd hoped they'd have been.
Three days you've done it, three days! – Thank God.
Three days you've done it. Therefore you nod

And know you can do it another week through,
Another, another, and then maybe two.
You've made a change in your life – just a bit!
And this time you know that you won't just quit

As you've done so often before
Because you hadn't kept up the score
Of the promises made on New Year's Day,
Which are good to make, or so they say.

So now is it possible for you to see
How very much better life can be
When you look at it realistically
And set your goals accordingly?

God still smiles and blesses you
For every single thing you do
That brings you closer in line with God's will,
Little by little and a little more still.

Adding Prayer

Want to add prayer to your life as a rule?
Want to add lots and not seem a fool?
You can add it gradually
Instead of making it overwhelming seem.

If you truly want to start
To pray to God right from your heart,
To carve a niche for God in your life,
You don't have to play the harp and the fife.

Here's one thing that you may want to try
Because time and life seem to fly by:
Every once in a while, every now and then,
Stop; stand still; count to five or to ten;

And while you do that, say, "God, here I am;
They tell me that you here with me stand.
Thank you; but now again I must rush
And get back here into this crush."

This only took five seconds or ten,
And maybe you sped through your "prayer" even then
And forgot all about it 'til after the end
Of that long day and thought not again

Of God, to whom you'd just "tipped your hat,"
Until the next day – or the day after that.
And then you found yourself upset
That you'd forgotten your best friend yet.

But God says to you, "That's the longest time
You have given me just to be mine
In years and years and years before.
I look forward to five seconds more."

That itself, God's message to you,
Took another five seconds, it's true.
But, wait. Did it take – or give – to you
That gift of time, though seconds few?

More and more often you may find
Five-second-long periods of time
When you remember God's there with you
And that God will always see you through.

What you find so special that occurs
Is that those first seconds you endured
Silent, alone, praying to God,
Eventually become a constant good.

[It only happens because you aim for 5 seconds and succeed. It won't happen if you aim for 1 hour and fail! In that case you might not try very often again, if at all. Start easy and build and grow. If you put enough five-second periods together end-to-end, they become forever!]

The Epiphany Star

The star shows the way.
The wise ones visit.
Precious gifts are given.
An even more precious gift
Is received
And welcomed
Into the world,
And lives are changed.

The star points the way
To the true Light of the World.
Will we look?
Will we find?
Will we welcome?
Will we receive?
Will we trust?
Will we follow?
Or will we turn away?

The star still shines.
How will you respond – today?
Not yesterday, not tomorrow,
But today?
And how will I?

Moreover, will we journey with each other,
Or will we each try to go it alone?
I invite you to journey with me.

"The light shines in the darkness,
And the darkness has not overcome it."
(John 1:5, Holy Bible)

Karyl J. Leslie

Epiphany (January 6)

Epiphany – a manifestation.
Epiphany – a revelation.
Epiphany – a day of joy.
Epiphany – God's little boy.

Epiphany – a day of grace.
Epiphany – we see his face.
Epiphany – the magi come
Epiphany – to worship one

Whom God has sent to live with us,
Whom God has sent to lift us up,
Whom God has sent to save us from
The enemy who tries to come

And steal our joy and blessedness
And make our hearts and lives restless:
A trackless waste, no way made known
Unless we keep God on the throne.

Epiphany in January
Shows us God's great loving caring
Coming to earth to live with us:
Immanuel – God *is* with us.

The sixth day of January,
A day more blessed than ordinary,
Is when we know the coming of
The magi to see God's gift of love.

January starts a brand new year.
Our desks and calendars are clear,
Ready to receive from us
Instructions how to fill them up.

Let's follow in the magi's way.
Let's lift our voices, let us say
That God's Son has finally come
And the holy war has won.

Let's look and see the shining light.
Let's follow the star of hope so bright.
Let's make our goal each day we go
More and more the Lord to know.

Into our date books and schedules
Let us put the God who rules
And set aside some special time
To be with God and know we're fine.

No matter how our life may seem,
It surely isn't just a dream
That Christ has come and redeemed us.
Let's worship God and make a fuss

Over the great good news of Christ,
The one who shines God's holy light
In ways we've never known before.
Spend some time Christ to adore.

Karyl J. Leslie

Light in Darkness

May the blessed Light that shines in darkness
Fill you through and through
And guide you every day
In all that you may do.

Angels – Messengers of God

I thought of an angel
And what did I do?
I thought of an angel
Blessing you.
I thought of an angel
And in my own mind,
I saw that that angel
Was remarkably kind.

What angel? You say.
No angels around.
They fly in the sky
Not bless on the ground.
But, oh, my friend, oh
Don't snicker and snort
For angels are everywhere
And of every sort.

Do you hate to be blessed?
I guess some people do.
Do you hate to bless others?
What good you could do
If you would reach out
A heart or a hand.
You might just help someone
Learn how to stand.

If we all pull together
What blessings there'd be,
If we don't just grouch
And cast stones – one, two, three.
I thought of an angel
And what did I do?
I thought of an angel.
It was blessing you.

Karyl J. Leslie

Snow Bird

The snow falls.
Birds hide.
Little footprints
By and by
Are seen
So delicate.

You follow them
To the tree
And, looking up,
You can see
Two small eyes
Peeking down.

Little birdie
In the tree,
I see you,
And you see me.
Can we
Become friends?

Little bird,
You, who fly,
Can you see
God in the sky?
I try, too,
Like you.

Seasons

I like to walk in the sunshine;
I like to walk in the rain.
The sun is warm upon my head;
Raindrops wet my hair.

I like to see the snowflakes fall
And to catch them on my tongue.
I like to see the leaves turn red
And jump in piles of them.

Spring or summer, winter or fall:
Which is my favorite season of all?
I do like each and every one.
In them all I can have fun.

Karyl J. Leslie

An Order for Worship

God says: I love you – deeply.
I care.
We respond with
THE ADORATION OF GOD.

God says: I love you – deeply.
I care.
Talk to me.
We respond with
THE CONFESSION OF SIN.

God says: I love you – deeply.
I care.
Believe.
We respond with
THE AFFIRMATION OF FAITH.

God says: I love you – deeply.
I care.
Go and do likewise.
We respond with
THE DEDICATION OF LIFE.

In the Beginning

In the beginning
There was God.
God created us
And loved us
And wanted us
To turn to God,
To love God,
To want to be
With God.

In the beginning
Was God.
We are not supreme.
We are not in charge.
We cannot even love
As God wants us to love.
But in the beginning
God was there.

From the beginning
God has heard
And answered prayer.
God has reached to us;
And when we find
We cannot make it
On our own,
We finally
Come to our senses
And grasp the hand
God's held out to us
For so long.

Snowstorm

It's snowing out. The sky is gray.
Snowflakes fall in quick array
And take their places on the ground
And spread their whiteness all around.

The cars are covered inches deep.
The cold can make one want to weep
If one goes out without one's gloves
Or inadequately covers up.

It's a great day to stay inside.
You might feel like you want to hide
Under the bedcovers, fast asleep.
Appointments you don't want to keep

Because it would mean going out
And getting cold without a doubt
Unless you shovel very fierce
And make the sweat your shirtsleeves pierce.

I will stay in for the day
And some music gladly play
While I do some work inside
And warm myself with tea beside.

Enjoy the day now, if you can,
Even if it changes plans
Of what you had in mind to do.
Be assured, you will get through.

With heated homes and lamps alight
We need not spend the day in fright
But celebrate the gifts we have.
If we do, the day's not bad.

Ordained

Today's my anniversary.
I was ordained this day
So many long, long years ago,
And this is what I say:

Thank you, God, for blessing me
With laying on of hands
And leading me to ministry
In places that weren't grand,

Nor were the places glorious,
But full of your good folk.
We worked together in your name,
Sometimes sharing a joke.

We laughed and cried and sang and prayed
As year went on to year.
My goal was always, as I went,
To bring a little cheer.

But sometimes I too needed
A touch of heavenly grace,
And sometimes I would see you
In a gently smiling face.

My goal was not "the ministry"
As a sole worker then.
I sought to serve with people
Who had you as a Friend,

To help others to know you
And your amazing love
Which showers us with blessings
Daily from above,

As well as from the depths of life.
Blessings are there, too;
And if someone believes it,
Miracles shine through.

So as today I celebrate
My anniversary,
I reflect on these past years,
Where God's face I do see.

Thank you, all, for blessing me
With your lives and your work.
Thank you that your faithfulness
To God you did not shirk.

February Readings

God's Love A-Z

A manger was the birthplace of the Christ Child.
Before God came to us in Christ, God sent prophets.
Christ was the human manifestation of the Divine Being.
Daily God dwells with us in Spirit and fact.
Every home can welcome God in Christ as they welcome strangers in Christ's Name,
For God loves every being God has created.
God looks with divine favor upon each one.
Hasty retreat from God's Holiness is not what God demands.
I know that because of God's overwhelming love.
Just as God foretold through prophets,
Kindness is what is on God's heart even when God is angry.
Love sometimes dictates that consequences must be faced.
Most often, though, it is mercy that reigns through God's forgiving love.
Nothing can separate us from God's love in Christ.
Only we can turn away from God, but still
Plenty of people try to ration the quantity or quality of God's love for themselves or others.
Qualms they have about accepting the wholeness and breadth of that love.
Restlessly, some seek to fill their lives with good deeds,
Seeking to win or earn God's approval.
Trusting God's eternal, irrepressible love is hard sometimes
Unless one opens one's heart and one's mind and one's spirit and one's very life.
Virtue does not win God's love but results from it.
Wait upon the Lord; attend to God's holy Presence.
e**X**pect miracles to happen when you let God's love flow and overflow.
Young and old, rich and poor, and all who are in between,
Zealously God loves you – and all. Zealously respond.

Karyl J. Leslie

Winter

Winter cold
And bitter winds
Can chill our bones
And freeze our skins
Unless we have
A warmth inside
That melts the ice
Which in us lies.

Winter can be
A state of mind,
An attitude,
Not just a time
Of year that comes
With frost and snow
While icy winds
Around us blow.

We all have times
Of cold within
When hearts feel like
They're made of tin,
And we just can't
Give out our love
Until the spring
Comes from above.

God's always there
To melt our sins
And thaw the freeze
We feel within;
So we can love,
Reach out again.
When warmth returns
We've touched God's hand!

A Fact of Life

This I know:
We all must go
Into the land of despair
Where we learn to bear
Each pain and fear
While no one else is near.

We come out
Stronger no doubt
For the pain we suffered there,
While learning to care
More about the other
Treating each as sister/brother.

Karyl J. Leslie

Happy Valentine's Day

I want to wish you on this day
All the love and joy and play
That can be found on Valentine's Day
Because you're special in many ways.

Peace and love and joy divine:
May these be yours; may they be mine,
Whether or not you choose to dine
On special foods or treats designed

To make it feel a special day.
And, as this greeting comes your way,
I lovingly to you do say,
Have a happy Valentine's Day.

To My Friend...

Peace. Solitude. Meditation. Sharing. Caring.
Watching the fire glow and warm.
Watching the dusk draw near.
Feeling the depth of life around.
And wishing you were here!

Wonderful Worship

I'm waiting now to go to church
Where in my seat I'll take my perch
So I can soar to worlds unknown
In Spirit at the Father's throne.

There's not much more I can do, though,
Before I must put on my coat
And get into my car so cold
And drive to church where there is gold:

Gold in glowing spirits there,
Gold in faces bowed in prayer,
Gold in gems of wisdom from
The Word of God proclaimed in song,

In story, and in poetry.
God's voice is heard in all the three
If we open our hearts to hear
And let God's Word take good root there.

A word of love we do proclaim.
Nothing needs to be the same
As it would be without the gift
Of love which hearts and spirits lift.

Worship is a wondrous thing
Where people all their praises bring
To offer God, who reigns on high,
But who stays also very nigh.

The sound of songs and voices raised
In giving God eternal praise
Is one I do not like to miss.
It represents dear heaven's bliss.

And so I love to go to church
And with others take my perch
As we worship God on high,
Who is also very nigh.

Heaven kisses us and we kiss back.
In doing this there is no lack
Of hope that in our hearts can rise,
Trusting God, Lord of the skies,

Of earth and heaven Sovereign.
There is no one to God foreign,
For all are God's creations dear,
Whether for God they cheer or sneer.

Let's be those who cheer and praise.
Let's be those whose voices raised
In song and laughter and in prayer
Seek God's mercy everywhere.

Karyl J. Leslie

A Lovely Time of Worship

I went to church this morning.
I had a lovely time
Of worshiping my Maker
And singing hymns that rhyme.

Brand New Day

Today I rested off and on.
I was up before the dawn.
The night was long, I lay awake
It seemed all night, for goodness' sake.

I didn't want to work right then
So I sat with a marking pen
And colored in a coloring book.
A little time, that's all it took

For me to feel relaxed and free
From the awful tyranny
Of stressful thoughts and anxious dreams.
Simple things are what it seems

To take sometimes when things seem rough,
When we want to hang in tough
Against the ghosts and goblins that
Remind us of a painful past.

So freely now I can go on
And put aside whatever's wrong
For the remainder of the night
Until day dawns with morning light

And hearts resume remembering
The wonders God in each day brings,
And life is made brand new again.
For now let's say, "Thanks, God. Amen."

God Be With You

May the light of Christ enfold you
As you live from day to day.
May the love of God still hold you
When you cannot find your way.
May you trust the resurrection
Even when the winter's dark.
May you always hear the angels sing
As they summon you to "hark"
And listen to the word of God
As it brings hope upon your way.
May you shine with Christ's own holy light
In all you do and say.

A Teddy Bear Song

Teddy bear, Teddy bear, in the night,
Why do your eyes seem to gleam so bright?
Is it with dreams dancing in your head?
What do you see when I go to bed?

Do you see visions of angels at play?
Do you hear songs on their harps today?
Or do they play on trumpets so loud
You can hear them above any crowd?

Do you feel warm and fuzzy inside
When my eyes close and in bed I lie?
You bring me comfort, so warm and so nice.
I love to have you right here by my side.

Teddy bear, Teddy bear, in the night,
Why do your eyes seem to gleam so bright?
Is it with love you feel through and through?
Do you know how very much I love you?

Teddy bear, Teddy bear, I love you so.
I am so glad you didn't say no
When I invited you here by my side.
You didn't turn away and didn't go hide.

You snuggle close to me in the night
Helping me to deal with the fright
I feel sometimes when the bad dreams come.
You then are my comforter, number one.

I see you lying here by me.
Calm, cool, collected you seem to be.
Because of your calmness, I am calm, too.
I really love lying here beside you.

Teddy bear, Teddy bear, day and night,
I love to hug you and hold you so tight.
Even though you are just a stuffed bear,
Because of you I know my folks care.

They quickly said yes when I picked you out.
I didn't have to scream or shout
To get them to buy you and bring you on home.
With you around, I don't feel alone.

Teddy bear, Teddy bear, in the night,
Why do your eyes seem to gleam so bright?
Is it with dreams dancing in your head?
I love that you're here with me in my bed.

Ash Wednesday

Ash Wednesday comes, and thus
Begins the time of Lent,
A period of forty days
When our time is spent
Preparing for an Easter
Of unsurpassing joy
Because we've taken this time
To refine our life's alloy.

During Lent we study
What the Bible says
And we apply it to our lives
To learn just what is meant
By loving God in fullness
And our neighbors as ourselves.
We look at all our actions
And find where sin has dwelt.

We each look at our own lives
To see if we can see
Where we've fallen short of this
And where our sins may be.
Count them up, the forty days,
And you may be surprised
To find that Sundays do not count
As days of Lent's denial.

For Sunday is the day, you know,
When Christ rose from the dead,
And every Sunday is a day
To celebrate. Instead
Of looking at our failures,
We view Christ's victory,
The death and resurrection
That set God's people free.

So on Sundays we do not fast
And look dismally upon
The ways we've fallen short,
The things that we've done wrong.
Instead we simply celebrate
Christ's holy victory
When God raised him up from the dead
And set our spirits free.

So don't forget this Lenten time
To take Sundays as a break;
And remember what Christ did,
All for sinners' sake.
The battle has been fought now.
The victory's been won,
And we can look upon our sins
And know in Christ they're gone.

While it's important to look
And see where we might change
Our lives and hearts and imaginings
In a holier range,
We yet must still remember
That nothing's come to pass
That can take the love of God away,
Which in Christ does last

From day to day in this life
And through eternity.
As you face Lent this year,
Plan to be set free
From all that has enslaved you
Or bound you deep in sin.
Let Christ's holy light in
And break into a grin.

For Christ loves you immensely,
And with the Spirit's proof
Will show you the most precious
Part of God's own truth.
Observe Lent as you choose to.
Deny yourself or not,
But let it be a time that
You let Christ cleanse each spot,

Each blot and every blemish
Upon your harried life,
And never more be burdened
With that sense of strife,
Fighting with yourself
About whether God cares.
In Christ's resurrection,
Let's get ourselves prepared

And lay aside each worry,
Each burden of remorse,
And let Christ's blood now cleanse you
Over the lake and moors.
For Christ loves you sincerely
And died so you might live.
God raised him up in victory
And showed love always wins.

Retirement

It's high noon, and here I sit
Wanting to make a go of it,
But there are things to figure out,
So many that I want to shout.

I need to figure out some things,
For every day a challenge brings
Until I get things sorted out
And know what life is all about

In this new state of "retiredness."
I pray the time will be quite blessed
And that I'll finally live my life
Without some of the former strife

That took place in my mind and heart
As each day I would take my part
In the world of full-time work.
I'd tried so hard not to shirk

My duties as I lived each day.
I hardly took much time to play,
But I made sure each day to pray
That God would show me just the way

God wanted me to use my life;
And now without the workday strife,
I still ask God to show me how
God wants to shape my new life now.

March Readings

Glory

Glory to our God above.
All around we see God's love.
Seeing yet is not enough:
We must learn how to stand tough
Against the evil close at hand
Spreading far across the land.

We must trust God's love and will
And learn to follow, yes, until
The time does come when Love shall win
Over every trace of sin.
From that day God's glory will shine
Ever brightly for all time.

We will see, and we will know
How much our sin and pain below
Greatly grieve God's heart above,
Which aches to give us all such love.
Finally we'll truly feel
God's love for us as truly real.

Karyl J. Leslie

Lenten Theme

On a Wednesday last month
We met – quite a bunch
Of us during the evening time.

We thought and we prayed,
We sang and we stayed
To consider the cost that was paid

For our freedom and mirth,
Our renewal, rebirth,
As hopeful creatures of God.

We met with each other
And tried not to shudder
At what we would find up ahead;

For Jesus did go
Through pain so we'd grow
Into spiritual progress and light.

He lived and he died,
He laughed and he cried
Because of his love for us all.

But death sure was not
The end of the plot
That God had in store for God's Son.

Through temptation and trial
Christ did trust all the while
That God was the One he would laud.

He'd never submit,
Not one little bit,
To a rival who hated his God,

The One true and only
Help of the lonely,
The best companion there is.

Jesus walked on this earth
To bring us to birth
As children of God's holy love.

With power and grace
He'd look at our face.
His eyes would shine with a glow.

Was it a tear?
He holds us dear.
Now isn't that something to know?

And what do you do,
Do you have a clue
What Jesus wants for your life?

It's time to return
To the heart that does burn
With the greatest love that there is.

For God gave God's Son,
The true holy One,
To bear our sins on the cross.

He suffered and died.
Have you ever tried
To thank him for such depth of grace?

And next month, it's true,
We'll see something new,
For Christ will rise from the dead.

He gives unto us
Life without fuss
And ado and worry and such.

For if we trust in him
We always will win
The battle for right against wrong.

So during these days
Of Lent, let's just praise
Jesus Christ, Son of God.

Let's join in the fun
That comes when we've done
What we feel God is calling us to.

May your Lenten journey
Be without hurry
And bless you and rest you in God.

May the Tempter lose power,
For every hour
God is with you, is right by your side.

Don't worry and fret.
In peace won't you let
Jesus walk right by your side?

He's with you today
And he'll always stay
And be the very best guide.

A Truth

You aren't really true until you learn:
You don't really live unless you love,
You don't really give unless you care,
You aren't really real without concern.

KARYL J. LESLIE

On Suffering

Why do we suffer?
That is the question.
Why all this pain?
What is the lesson?

Do we deserve
What happens to us?
We can't see how,
And it bothers our trust.

Our trust in God
When we don't know the plan
Is hard for each one –
Child, youth, woman, or man.

So, why do we suffer?
That is the question.
Is it frailty of flesh
Or some other reason?

Can it be simply
A matter of will:
Someone promoting
Their will though it kills?

God's blessings abound
In spite of the fuss.
Could it be Satan
Is just testing us,

Trying to get us
To deny our faith,
To turn from Christ
And not care that we're saved?

Whatever the reason,
No one's exempt.
Is it a matter of
How well we repent?

No, it is not.
God's mercy and grace
Are offered to all,
Whatever the case.

Suffering, suffering,
It happens to all.
Pain and great hardship:
On whom can you call?

Don't look to a genie
From out of a bottle.
Just rest in God.
In Christ's arms God's got you.

In Whose Eyes?

I looked at my life for a while.
Some memories could make me smile.
Others brought regret and loss.
I'd lived through them but at a cost.

So I turned my face to God,
Who lifted me from where I trod
In the mires of shame and grief,
Bringing me some great relief.

Often we feel very low
When we think of chances blown.
We walk the earth with low esteem
But God holds for us a great dream,

Not of what we do ourselves,
Not of trophies on our shelves,
But of what God can do for us
When we let go so much fuss.

God's dream is what we might become
If we follow God's way home.
God lifts us up from self-defeat
To a vision that's quite neat.

So if you think you're not worth much,
See yourself with God's own touch
Imprinted on your heart and soul,
And know that God can make you whole.

For worth is not in human flesh.
Worth is in our spirits, drenched
In the garb of God's own love,
Clothed in blessings from above.

Kite-Flying

In a day of peace and gladness,
In a moment of sheer madness,
I can take my kite and let it fly,
And with it see my spirit try
To express to all the world around
The freedom it has finally found.

Joining In

Dear Brothers and Sisters in Christ,
I think that it's all very nice
That we say we believe,
But can we conceive
Of the fullness of God's grace tonight?

The seeds of grace surely abound
Every time we rejoice in the sound
Of God's Holy Word
And the stories we've heard
That set us on blessed fertile ground.

Let's learn every day something new
As we learn every day what to do.
We can study the Word
And share what we've heard
In new insights for me and for you.

Group study, prayer, worship, and more
Should not be too big of a chore
To express our embrace
Of God face to face
And to show just how much we adore.

So let's go to the party that's church.
Do you know what your presence is worth,
Not just to those there,
But to God, who does care?
Let us go, and let's shake up the earth.

Stormy Weather

When the storms rage all around you,
I'll be there.
When the storms rage all around you,
I'll be there.
When the boat is tossed about,
There's no need to weep or shout.
When the storms rage all around you,
I'll be there.

When the wind and rains are heavy,
I'm with you.
When the wind and rains are heavy,
I'm with you.
When the wind and rains assail you,
Know my strength will never fail you.
When the wind and rains are heavy,
I'm with you.

If your mind is filled with chaos,
Turn to me.
If your mind is filled with chaos,
Turn to me.
When your thoughts all whirl around,
Know that peace can yet be found.
If your mind is filled with chaos,
Turn to me.

When it seems that life is worthless,
Call on me.
When it seems that life is worthless,
Call on me.
When your strength is all used up,
Come and share my bread and cup.
When it seems that life is worthless,
Call on me.

I will give you a new vision,
Yes, indeed.
I will give you a new vision,
Yes, indeed.
There is hope and there is peace
When I give you sweet release.
I will give you a new vision,
Yes, indeed.

O come to me, my children,
Come to me.
O come to me, my children,
Come to me.
When you come to me, my friends,
I'll give peace that never ends.
O come to me, my children,
Come to me.

Guidance

I don't really want to do this now.
What would I rather do?
I'm not sure anything appeals.
I'm stumped now without you –

Without you, God, to guide me,
To give me your advice,
But even when you give it,
I'm not always so nice,

To listen and to heed you,
To follow where you lead.
Instead I'd rather isolate
Myself in my own need.

My CD player isn't
Helping me just now,
Because it won't play anything.
It's broken down somehow.

I miss the background music
That was five CD's full
Of music praising you, God.
My spirit it did pull

Toward the God of love we have
Who holds us in God's care
Even when we turn away
And aren't at all aware

Of God's ever-present love,
The hope we have each day,
For bad dreams surely will not
Have the final say

Of who we are, what we're about,
Or what's in store for us.
We have God's promises that stand
In spite of all the fuss.

God's promises are timeless.
They'll never fail, but we
At times are very stubborn
And refuse their good to see.

We'd rather keep our minds on
The pressures that we face
Than rest our hearts in Jesus
And God's loving embrace.

Let's turn around. Let's all repent
And face away from sin.
Let's look to God and let the radiance
Of God's love shine in

And brighten up our little lives
And make us wonder-filled
As we worship the One who
Wants our lives fulfilled.

Smile

Smiles may help you in many ways
If you use them throughout your days.
Although to you your smile looks sappy,
It might make other people happy.

If you wear a smile today
You may just brighten another's day.
If she happens to try to thank you,
You will know why she's not blue.

Are you bothered by a bully?
Go up to him and smile fully.
By this doing fairly often,
Him you might succeed to soften.

To find other purposes for the smile,
Use it often, try it all the while.
If you do not achieve results,
Keep trying!

"What Can Separate Us…?"

"If God is for us, who is against us?"

God loves us,
loves us more than we can ever know.
God loves us now,
standing here,
early in the morning,
celebrating Life.

God loves us wherever we are,
whatever we do.
God's love never dies.
God wants what's good for us.
God wants us to be happy,
to have joy,
to love life.

God is always for us,
even when we aren't "for" ourselves.

"If God is for us, who is against us?"
If God is for us, who can take us from God?
If God is for us, who can separate us from
God's love?

Death didn't take God's love away from us,
even the death of God's Own on a cross,
hung there by God's people –
and all people are God's people.
God loves all even if they don't know
God exists,
even if they deny that God exists.

Nothing can separate us from God's love.
Even when we deny that God loves us,
the love is still there.
Even when we feel God has forsaken us,
God's love is still there;
that love still causes God to hurt for us,
to hurt *with* us.

God's love is forever.
God's love is now,
in every now,
now when you feel it,
now when you deny it;
in every moment
of every day
of your life;
in every activity,
in every rest,
of your life;
in every joy,
in every hurt,
of your life.

God's love is now.
God's love is forever.
God's love cannot be taken from us —
ever.

"If God is for us, who is against us?"

KARYL J. LESLIE

Springtime's Best

It's getting to be Springtime now;
The snow is soon to end.
The daylight hours are longer,
Warm weather's round the bend.

The robins have appeared once more.
They hop along the ground,
And early in the morning, you
Can hear birds' singing sound.

Daylight Savings Time has come.
We've turned our clocks ahead.
Morning darkness lingers, though,
When we get out of bed.

I look forward to the Spring,
But not the allergies.
And in Summer I don't care
At all for bugs and bees.

Each season has its pluses,
Even Wintertime.
Each also has its challenges,
Which are not hard to find.

Our task is to look for the good
And celebrate it well
And find a way just to relax
And maybe sit a spell

And ponder God's creation,
The wonder of it all,
And be amazed at all God's done
To show great love for all.

The Divine Holy Great One
Loves each of us so well
That Christ has come to save us
From the gates of hell.

Christ's Easter resurrection
Is the best thing about Spring,
So be sure you take some time
To laugh and pray and sing;

For God has promised to you
Eternal life as well.
Think of someone to whom
You can the Good News tell.

For God offers to all people
The chance to come on home
To a grand reunion
Around God's holy throne.

But we really have to want it.
We must R.S.V.P.
And say that we're rejoicing
God's glory soon to see;

Accept forgiveness offered,
Extend to all the same
In God's gracious holy love
And in Christ Jesus' name.

For you're invited with me
The banquet to attend
Where we will know God's mercy
And praise God without end.

Karyl J. Leslie

Rainstorm

It looks like it might rain tonight.
I hope it doesn't give me fright
With thunder loud and lightning bright.
I'd like to sleep in peace this night.

April Readings

Palm Sunday

Grab a palm branch, wave a flag.
Watch out for that rocky crag.
Christ the Lord has come to town.
Get a pencil. Write it down.

Let us have a grand parade.
Shout together, "Christ has made
Many people well again.
He is surely heaven-sent."

Karyl J. Leslie

Holy Week: Monday

Then on Monday hear him teach
Those who would for heaven reach,
Those who want to know God's will,
Those who seek, for good or ill,

To hear the words he has to say
And let them in their hearts have play
Until they have a sense of what
This One from God has truly brought.

Holy Week: Tuesday

Tuesday comes, and with it more
Teaching by the Temple's doors.
Learn from Jesus Christ the way
Heaven's laws thus to obey.

Time is getting closer now
For the ultimate showdown
Between the One who comes from God
And those who reign on human sod.

Karyl J. Leslie

Mandatum (Maundy/Holy Thursday)

Maundy Thursday – mandatum.
Mandate. Commandment.
"A new commandment
I give to you,
That you love one another.
Just as I have loved you,
So you must love one another
And thus show yourselves
To be my disciples."
Not condoning bad behavior
Or ignoring it
But setting higher standards.
Serving
One another.
As I have
Served you.
Mandatum. Mandate.
Commandment.
Love.
Not a feeling
But a choice,
A decision,
A will,
And a willingness
To forgive
To challenge
To restore
To uphold
And to assist.
To give
And to receive
Graciously
Gracefully

Gratefully
With thanks.
Maundy Thursday.
Washing
Breaking bread
Sharing drink
Historic memories
A memorial
A remembrance
A re-membering
Making real
Making present
Real Presence
Holy Supper
Shared conversation
Spoken words
Hidden thoughts.
All are there:
The betrayer –
But so much more.
The denier –
But so much more.
One later called "Doubting" –
But so much more.
The deserters,
Those who ran,
Those who slept,
Those who loved
But didn't know how
Or how much
They loved
Or were loved
Until later –
Much later,
And not so much later.

All were there.
Heard the words.
Saw the acts.
Felt the deep, deep love
But maybe were
Too embarrassed
To realize or admit it.
Women? Children?
We are not told,
But probably.
Possibly?
It was a family affair.
A child would ask
The questions of the night.
Passover.
A celebration.
A memorial.
A retelling.
A re-membering.
A longing for home.
Maundy Thursday.
Mandatum. Commandment.
Mandate.
A new commandment
I give to you:
Love one another.
Just as I have loved you,
So you must love one another.
Thus you will show
That you are
My true disciples.
Love
One
Another.
As I have

Loved you
And *do* love you
And *will* love you
To the very end,
And to the utmost,
The nth degree,
Beyond anything
And everything.
Yes, you:
The betrayer.
Yes, you:
The doubter.
Yes, you:
The denier.
Yes, you:
The sleepers.
Yes, you:
The deserters.
Come to me,
And learn from me,
And you will find rest
For your souls.
A new commandment:
Love.

Karyl J. Leslie

Why Do They Call It Good?

It's Friday now; the crowds are gone.
The Sabbath day has just begun.
The stars are out, the moon is dark.
Something's happened that's left a mark.

Jesus of Nazareth today,
The Savior of the world some say,
Was crucified a common man.
Just like the others', his blood ran

Down from wounds in hands and feet
And where the thorny crown did meet
His head that bowed with sorrow great.
I wouldn't want to have his fate.

Religious leaders didn't like
The way he gathered crowds in spite
Of their teachings and warnings dire.
They tried to squelch this leader's fire.

But Jesus went with willing feet
To the hill on which defeat
Seemed to have the last sad word.
From his disciples naught was heard.

They'd run away during the night.
They almost went without a fight,
But one of them did draw his sword.
He received a scolding word

From the one for whom he fought,
From the one whose life he sought
To protect from them that came.
Life would never be the same

Without that figure, that one of God,
The one they thought the Son of God.
He'd shown them wonders and signs galore;
And now in death he was no more.

Sorrowful now, they closed their eyes.
The darkness was a thin disguise
Which hid their faces from the rest.
They sobbed, each one, on their own breast.

How could this have happened here?
They'd lost their leader, O so dear.
For three years they'd followed him,
But now all hope had grown quite dim.

Crucified! They'd heard the nails
As they were pounded into frail
Flesh that had been beaten sound.
They heard but made sure they weren't found.

"Alas! And did my Savior bleed."
Alas! It was for my misdeeds.
My sins alone sent him to die.
My prayers and cries rise to the sky.

I mourn for him who died for me.
He died so I myself could be
Free for all eternity.
What is there that I can't see?

I can't see hope, I can't see trust,
But even so it's time I must
Pull myself together again
And wait upon God's holy plan

To show itself in its full ways.
Otherwise each of my days
Will go by so grim and drear.
I really need my Savior here.

But it is Friday. It is night.
I shiver in the cold with fright.
Does anyone else know my pain?
Were those three years all in vain?

I must lie down as my heart pounds.
I listen for any distant sounds
That mean they've come for me right here,
And that they'll take me in despair.

I leave my bed; I cannot sleep.
I cannot find a way to keep
The sights I saw and sounds I heard
From making me cry at the words

That I heard the Master say:
"It is finished." Thus the day
Ended with this cry of cries.
My broken heart in my chest lies.

And now upon the Sabbath day,
We must rest and think and pray,
And hope that as the Lord did say,
He'd rise again on the third day.

Comparatively Speaking (Good Friday)

My back hurts – but his hurt more.
His was something more than sore.
He'd been beaten, whipped, you see,
Flogged and scourged 'til all bloody.
A bloody mass was his back,
Not because of his own lack,
But because our sin he took,
And even then we all forsook
Him and fled away in fear.
Now we see it's very clear
We left him there to die alone,
Though seconds from God's holy throne
And hordes of angels who would fly
To rescue him if he would cry
To them to come and lift him up,
But he endured that bitter cup
Of suffering for you and me.
Look. What do you really see?
A sigh, a sign, a wayward crook
Or one who in his body took
The punishment that we deserved?
With what vision are you served
As you look upon him there
Stripped, exposed, and nearly bare?
Humiliation they desired
As they hung him there quite tired
From a sleepless night at best.
Could you or I have stood the test?
Or would we, too, have run away
And hidden locked in disarray;
And what about the great dismay
We felt as hopes just drained away
With the blood that from him flowed?

Was this some secret, holy code?
No, he was really dead and gone.
Now how could we, who'd loved, go on?
And so we huddled, locked in fear
That imprisoned us, yes, it's clear,
Beyond what earthly peril could.
We were shaking mighty good.
The Sabbath came, and he had died.
We broke down and deeply cried.
It was the end of what we'd known
And all the hope we'd had had flown
Away and left us in despair.
We felt all alone, though there
Were still eleven men here now,
And women, too, who'd been around
Ministering to his needs
As he did his holy deeds.
Some were going to the tomb.
They longed to go, oh, just as soon
As they could possibly do so.
They observed the Sabbath, though;
Then when it ended, they made haste
To the tomb. No time to waste.
But we did sit in this dark room
Full of thoughts of empty gloom.

It's Sunday now. Does the sun shine?
Will it ever again in time?
We have lost our dearest friend
And with his death did our hopes end.
We wait. We don't know what to do.
Can you feel our gloom all through
Your soul into the depths of it?
Will you with us watch and sit?

Good Friday Poem

Imagine how the disciples felt
That Friday night as they knelt
By their beds to pray to God.
It just seemed so very odd
That they were not together now,
That they had all run off somehow,
Away from Jesus in the night.
The guards had come. There was such fright.

The guards took Jesus away with them
While all His beloved disciples ran
To get away, to save their lives,
But now it didn't seem quite right.
Jesus, their Lord was crucified.
Peter said he'd even lied
And told the ones around that he
Didn't know the man, times three.
He denied that he knew Him.
He was wracked with grief and sin.

Then, "Crucify!" was the cry
From the crowd that gathered nigh,
Near to the ruler Pilate's place.
Of joyful crowds there was no trace
At that time to comfort Him.
There was neither friend nor kin
As Jesus stood, mocked, derided,
While the priests were so delighted
To hear the crowd call for Christ's death.
They felt relieved, now held no breath.

Christ was wounded, bruised, and flogged.
His mind was clear, there was no fog
To lighten the pain that came His way.
To defend Himself He didn't assay.

Led to the hill called Golgotha,
Known also as Place of the Skull.
Together with two criminals
Christ was hung on a cross on that hill.

Crucified, condemned to die.
His followers would wonder why,
Why had this Teacher so godly
Come to be nailed upon the tree?
It was jealousy which drove them all
To dare the deed, to have the gall
To put the Lord of life to death.
They didn't know the height nor depth
Of the love God had for *them*.
They were not excluded then
When Christ called out from on the cross,
"Forgive them, Father, or they'll be lost.
They do not know the meaning of
This act of faith, this gift of love
That I perform on their behalf.
Forgive them, Father, as they laugh
And mock and jeer with whistles clear
The Son of God, whom they should hear."

Friday night, He's dead and gone.
How, O how, could they go on?
He's buried in a tomb, you see,
With a large stone rolled to seal
The tomb closed. It is the end.
Why did they all abandon their friend
In His time of desperate need?
Now they could not eat or feed
Anything but their thoughts tonight.
They close their eyes. They close them tight,
But even so they see the sight
That should not have been, that was not right.

Sabbath has come the evening of
The day of the failure of their love
For their Lord, so dear, so dear.
Now they huddle alone in fear.
Will the authorities be after them?
Would they all be crucified then?

"It is finished!" Jesus had cried
Not long before He finally died,
Tortured long and hard and deep.
How could the disciples ever sleep
This night away until the morning?
Was this just a hideous warning
That they were next if they didn't watch out?
They'd better hide and not go out.

The Sabbath is over, a day of rest,
A day to think about the best
And the worst of what had happened
In the life that had been flattened,
Crucified, a horrible death,
And even so, with a pained breath
Jesus had said to one beside Him
That if he believed he would find him-
Self with Him in paradise,
The man on the cross who opened his eyes
And saw who Jesus truly was
And asked Him without any fuss
To remember him when He came to power
In God's realm that very hour.

Sunday morning dawns. They hear
Some women went so very near
To the tomb at early dawn,
And they saw the stone was gone

From the mouth of the tomb now open.
They could not think, but they were hopin'
That what Jesus said had come to pass,
That He would rise and at the last
Come to them, be seen again.
But it was too early to begin to grin.

Where was His body, where was He
Whom they had come so early to see?
An angel spoke, and to them said,
"He is not here. He is not dead."
And before you know it the women fled
To tell the others what he'd said.
It could not be true is what they thought;
That line of thinking they hadn't bought.
So Peter and John ran to the tomb
And found it empty of the One whom
They had followed so faithfully.
They scratched their heads and began to believe.

Jesus Christ was truly alive!
What a blessing - or did someone connive
To take the body away from there
And give them each a royal scare?
No, it was true! He appeared to them
And explained the facts once again,
That He would die and on the third
Day rise up and fulfill the word
God had spoken through the prophets
That none could slow, that none could stop it,
But that He died for your sins and mine,
And now in God's eyes we are fine,
Forgiven one, and forgiven all.
Now we must respond to the call
Day in, day out to live in Christ,

To let Him in deep in our lives,
To welcome Him to live within us.
He died in order that He might win us
Forgiveness from God and life anew.
Now what are *you* going to do
About the fact that He's alive
And yearns and longs to live inside
And through and with your very self?
Will you put Him on a shelf
And wait for some other day to arrive
Before with Him you become alive?

I ask you now. Tell the truth.
Do you accept His life as proof
That God seeks you to be God's own
And for you some day to come home
To God and dwell with God for life?
No longer are you two in strife
Against each other, for now you can
Be whole and clean and pure again,
For the victory Christ did win.
Let Him, O please let Him in.

Imagine how the disciples felt
That Friday evening as they knelt
By their beds to pray to God
As with tears they sobbed and sobbed.
But they have new life and so can you.
You know what you have to do.
Invite the risen Christ to come in
And cleanse your life from every sin.

Make the decision, make it now
And tell God that your heart you'll bow
And let Christ Lord and Savior be
So you can live eternally
With God in right relationship
Even though sometimes you'll slip.

Receive the gift, the gift divine.
Do it now, make this the time
That you say yes to God's great love.
Let us thank our God above.

The Waiting Game (Holy Saturday)

Holy Saturday, Holy God,
This day is one that's really odd.
Jesus Christ, from Mary's womb,
Now lies dead in a sealed tomb;

Or so it seems to those who wait
To see what will be their next fate.
Their Leader whom they'd followed for
Three long years – or were they short –

Was crucified just yesterday;
Yet all of them had run away
At his arrest the night before.
They now were feeling quite heart-sore.

They'd gathered now in fear and shame.
They barely dared to speak the name
Of the one to whom they'd given
All their hopes and dreams for livin'.

He'd sent them out once two by two
To do what God showed them to do.
So they'd gone out to do his work.
They'd healed the sick and taught his word.

They'd prepared the way for him
To go to towns he'd not yet been.
They had seen God's power in him,
But now they were at their wits' end.

What would they do now that he'd died?
They were still too shocked to cry.
Nonetheless their hearts were broken,
While they remembered words he'd spoken.

What in the world would they do now?
God would have to show them how
They could even go on living
Past the pain of their misgivings.

Nothing to do today but wait.
Although it's Sabbath, could they pray?
And if they did, what would they say?
Let us wait with them today.

Easter Greeting

Happy Easter to you;
May blessings abound.
May you find God's love
Always around.
It's Easter time now;
"Christ rose from the dead.
He now lives forever,"
God's kind angels said.

Christ Lives!

Easter morning,
Sad and bleak,
Women walking,
Him they seek.
Hope all gone and
Hearts bowed low.
Grief immense
Their hearts now know.

But, what is this?
They do not find
Their Savior there –
Or are they blind?
Where is now
His body dear?
They see it's now
No longer here.

Someone had come
Before the dawn
And taken his body
Which now was gone.
Despair piled up
Upon despair
Until they heard
Two voices there.

"He is not here.
Oh, don't you know?
What he had said
Has become so.
He is risen
From the dead.
See the cloth
From on his head.

See the grave clothes
Lying there.
He is risen!
Don't despair!
He lives again
And you will see
How he will give you
Lots of glee.

You will see him,
Hear his voice.
Tell the others
And rejoice!
He is always
With you now.
Celebrate
God's blessed pow'r."

We today,
So far along,
Sing the blessed
Easter song.
Our spirits soar
Because Christ lives.
New strength and hope
The Spirit gives.

Before the dawn
Of Easter day,
Things looked bleak,
But didn't stay
In darkness or
In sadness, for
Christ was raised
Forevermore!

Karyl J. Leslie

Easter Monday

Easter Monday is the day
We show forth in a sure way
What the Resurrection Day
Means for us from day to day.

New Life

The newness of spring,
The warmth of the sun,
All lead us to know
That new life can come.

May Readings

Thank You, God

Thank You, God, for this new day.
Thank You for gifts you send my way.
Thank You for life to live with You.
Thank You for everything You do.

Thank You for friends who know and care.
Thank You for being everywhere.
Thank You for helping when times are bad.
Thank You for helping me not to stay sad.

Karyl J. Leslie

My Artist Friend

God is an artist,
Painting the world
In many different hues.
We love the bright colors:
The reds and the yellows,
The greens and the blues;
But there are grays and blacks
That are painted there, too.
All work together to make the whole.
Thus it is also within my own soul:
I love the bright moments,
But how bright do they seem
Without those dark backgrounds
Against which to gleam?
My God is an artist
Within every soul:
The dark times and bright joys
Are in God's control.
We love the bright colors:
Your reds and my blues;
But let's take joy in dark moments
That God paints in there, too.

Colors of Life

In life so many colors
Spread their beauty through
The broad array of nature
And human beings, too.

We love the many colors.
Each one enriches life;
But sometimes with each other,
We're often choosing strife.

In politics and often
We try to say we're right
And all the others are wrong.
It makes a lively fight.

But in the world of nature
We admit variety's blessed.
With differences in color
We don't get all upset.

So in our lives with others
Let us try through and through
Not to divide our world
Into black and white, no blue.

No red, yellow, or orange,
No brown or green we see,
When we say that "Your thinking
Steers opposite from me."

Each person has opinions
We may not agree with,
But look for what is true there
And opportunity give

For each different person
To add to your worldview,
And let your whole perspective
Become a little new.

You want someone to listen
As you explain your thoughts.
Then you should listen to them.
You know you really ought.

They may be wrong on some things,
But they have the best intent.
You can disagree with them,
But hear just what they meant.

They see things from a different
Perspective, that is true,
But if you want them to listen,
Then you must listen, too;

And we'll enrich each other.
We'll add a blessing to
Someone we disagree with
When we say, "That's really true."

So as the season changes,
Let's open up our minds
And let our thinking grow up
As we agreement find.

Sometimes we have to look hard
To find it, that is true;
But there must still be something
About which I agree with you.

Although at times I disagree
With the view that you put forth,
May I still listen to you
And try to find some warmth,

Something you say that stretches me
Beyond my present view.
I'll respect that in you
If you respect me, too.

Let's try to love each other
And let minds sometimes change
And even with discomfort
Find a comfortable range

In which we can live together
As brothers, sisters true;
For God has placed you in my life
So you can enrich me, too.

Height

Away in the sky
Where the birds always fly
My spirit runs free
And wants to take me.

Above all the noise,
Above all the haste,
Where time fills with joys,
Not a moment is waste.

My heart wants to soar,
But the deafening roar
Of the pressures below
Just won't let it go;

While inside, my spirit
Knows God's voice
And does hear it.
God tells me to fly

Way up in the sky
Where the birds always go
And my heart God does know.
With God I will go.

A Gracious Nod

The light of Christ, O gracious God,
Shows to us your own dear nod
That though evil looks really strong,
Your love wins over every wrong.

With your goodness and your love,
You can lift our hearts above
Anything that tries to sink
Our spirits down beneath the brink.

For instance, on that Easter day,
Centuries ago and far away,
Angels rolled the stone away,
And resurrection had its say.

Christ was raised up from the grave,
Christ who lived and died to save
This whole sad world from sin and strife,
Christ who gave his very life.

And so, to him, new life you gave,
Nevermore to fade away.
Christ is with us every day.
Thanks and praise to you we pay.

This light of Christ, O gracious God,
Shows to us your own dear nod
That though evil sometimes looks strong,
You can turn our hearts to song.

Karyl J. Leslie

Hearty Belief

You say you believe in the Christ.
I say that believing is nice,
But sometimes it's not
Enough in tight spots
Just to believe when it's light.

To say we believe's not enough,
For our lives can get pretty tough.
So we must reinforce
The good things, of course,
And hold tightly when things do get rough.

Believing is not just for heads.
It's for hearts; it's for praying in beds.
It's for bodies and souls
And for making us whole
When we follow where Jesus Christ led.

Each of us has many needs,
But we often live more for our greeds.
There are treasures galore
In what God has in store
When we let God be the planter of seeds.

Put Jesus Christ right at the heart –
Now this would be very smart –
Of all that you do
And what you say, too,
And every day take up your part.

Believe in the one crucified,
Resurrected, and, yes, glorified.
Believe with your will.
Follow this one until
Your world has been reorganized.

Never Too Old

What would you like to be
When you grow up, my friend?
I ask not idle-ly,
I ask with good intent.

It does not matter how
Many birthdays you have spent
Getting where you are.
What's your new goal, my friend?

Or are you satisfied
With the you you have become,
And do you want to stay?
That could be so humdrum.

A new goal you can set,
A new phase enter in.
You could become a new
Woman or a new man.

For myself, I think
My prayer is to become
A much-loved child of God
Who's welcome in God's home;

But, wait a minute! Whoa!
That's already been done.
It is a given fact.
It's by God's grace alone

That you or I can be
So loved that God delights
In us whether our lives
Show fruit or bear a blight.

For God's love does come first
In every scheme of things.
God shows us on the cross
How much this love can sting.

God gave God's all for us
Because God loves us so.
We do not need to earn
That love which freely flows.

But that is not our way
With those we love, is it?
Don't we often ask
That they show some merit

Before we give our lives
So theirs might be enriched?
Or is that Satan's lie
To keep our minds bewitched?

Think of your own dear child,
The offspring that you love.
Was it first their worth
That taught you how to love?

Or was the love there first,
Pure and wholly good?
What did they do to earn
Your gift of daily food?

Can you see just how much
God must love you now
With love that comes before
You ever thought to bow

Before God's holiness
And great grand majesty?
God's love for you has been
Through all eternity.

Rise up now. Awake
With a new peace within.
Know that God is love.
The Scriptures tell us this.

Do not fret for yourself
Or your loved ones there,
For God will never cease
To shower you with care.

You may "mess up" at times.
It's true that we all do.
But God's great love for you
Will always see you through.

Some times may seem quite rough
When you stumble and fall;
But know that God's good grace
Can overcome it all.

What would you like to be
When you grow up, my friend?
It's already quite clear
You're loved without an end.

So set your mind to see
That you are not alone
And that you'll always be
Welcome at God's great throne.

Sacred Rest

I write in here today to say
It's been a long and tiring day,
But it has been refreshing, too,
With fulfilling things to do.

But I won't try to write much now.
I've other things to do somehow
To get into a relaxed mode
For when I put down this day's load

And go to rest my head a while
On pillows that help me to smile
When to bed I finally go
And hopefully into sleep flow.

So, "Good night," I will say for now
As ever later grows the hour.
I've done enough today so far.
I welcome the emerging stars

That signal that the night has come
And I am safely set at home.
I'll rest tonight with peaceful mind
And hope renewing dreams to find.

Peace to You

A song of peace I'd like to sing.
Peace upon this house I'd bring:
Peace of heart and mind and will,
Peace that leaves out conflict's chill;
Peace in spirit through God's love,
Peace that's grace from God above.

Bird Song

It was a gorgeous day today.
The sun shone forth in full array
Of brightness and of shadowed hues.
In the outdoors I kept amused
And tried to keep quite occupied,
Reveling in the warmth outside
While watching my sweet kitty cat
Bask in the window in my flat
Where he would watch the goings on
Of all the birds that sang their songs.
He enjoys his window seat.
For him it's quite a glorious treat
To sit or lie or roll around
Listening to that world of sound.

Truly Blessed

Blessed, happy, holy, healthy,
Fortunate indeed,
Are many whom the world considers
Stricken and in need:
The pure in heart, the poor in spirit,
Those who mourn and weep,
The ones who long for righteousness,
Who often cannot sleep
Because they spend their nights in prayer
To God, and ask God, "Please,
Bring your reign upon the earth
So we do as you please."

Blessed, happy, holy, healthy,
Fortunate indeed,
Are many whom the world considers
Stricken and in need.
The Son of Man himself, you know,
Was nailed upon the cross,
And most considered all he'd lived for
As a total loss.
But God has raised him up, you see,
To live again and reign.
He lives right now so we can know
Relief from broken pain.

Blessed, happy, holy, healthy,
Fortunate indeed,
Are many whom the world considers
Stricken and in need,
For they know God in richer ways,
Beyond imagining,
Than those who do not struggle now
Or hear the angels sing
Their sweet songs of freedom's joy

Beyond what we can know
Until we kneel at Christ's own feet
And in his presence go.

Blessed, happy, holy, healthy,
Fortunate indeed,
Are many whom the world considers
Stricken and in need.
Instead, rejoice, and be ye glad
In this great company,
And know that it is God's own face
That one day you will see –
A face of love, of righteousness,
Of grace and blessings, too,
For God has sent the only Son
To redeem me and you.

Blessed, happy, holy, healthy,
Fortunate indeed,
Are many whom the world considers
Stricken and in need.
We may be among them, too,
As we walk on this earth,
But in Christ's love we each can know
A new and holy birth;
And if we do, we can rejoice,
Very glad indeed,
For all the love that God has poured
Upon us in our need.

Blessed, happy, holy, healthy,
Fortunate indeed,
Are we even when we feel
Stricken and in need,
For God is there to comfort us,

To give us laughter new.
Let us follow Christ's own way,
The only way that's true.
We need him so, and we rely
On him for heart's content.
Therefore we, too, can sing with joy
Beyond this world's lament.

Blessed, happy, holy, healthy,
Fortunate indeed,
Can we be, too, when we may feel
Stricken and in need,
For we can know a Savior
Who lives our lives to bless
And who can take what we have made
A full and total mess
And turn it into something
That shines with God's light, too.
In response to God's great love,
It's the least that we can do.

Karyl J. Leslie

Retreat

I get to go to camp next month.
I think it will be fun.
We will get to see the stars,
The rising and the setting sun.

The brochure for the week says we
Will have a lot of fun,
And learn to know each other
As we share 'til day is done.

The birds will be out singing sweet.
The paths we'll walk are fine.
And if there isn't a clear path,
I'll make a way that's mine.

We'll study Bible and relate
To each other and to God;
And we may think no other place
Is as rich as what we've got.

We will not just be talking there.
We'll laugh and sing and play
And do a lot of different things
And for each other pray.

We can pray here or pray there
As steady as can be,
And we can pray using no words
While we God's glory see.

I'm glad that I have got the time
And opportunity
To share in this rich blessing
Along my life's journey.

June Readings

An Important Invitation

This is an important month,
Important in the year.
We hope that you will join with us
In praising God most dear.

On Sundays or in Bible School
We hope to see you soon.
Come and join us yet today,
For there is so much room.

Be with us, yes, abide with us,
Not only with God on high.
We pray that you yourselves
Will be often coming by.

We miss you when you're not with us
In worship and in prayer,
In fellowship and laughter, too,
So come by if you care.

We invest a lot in this.
Our prayers and lives we share.
But we want you to join with us
And fill the holy air

With songs of joy and songs of care,
With prayers and scripture, too.
You don't know what you're missing
When you don't come to God's school,

A school of life, a school of hope,
A school that teaches us
Everything we need to know
To live without a fuss.

We do not do things perfectly.
We're merely human, so
We sometimes slip and sometimes fall,
But God's love we surely know,

A love that reaches all of us,
A love that truly gives,
A love that lifts us from despair,
A love that so forgives

That we can lift our heads again,
And we can lift our hearts,
And joining with each other then
Can truly take our parts.

For we each have a part to play
To make the church be whole.
No one is extraneous,
No, not a living soul.

So come to join us as you are.
Our arms are open wide.
Do join us here in God's great love,
And meaning true you'll find.

Pentecost Day

Pentecost is a wonderful day,
a day of excitement and mirth.

Everyone come, enjoy this day,
the day of the church's birth.

Nearly two thousand years ago it was
the disciples had gathered as one.

The Holy Spirit came from above,
and now the church was begun.

Each was blessed in a special way;
the Spirit touched upon each,

Coming as wind and coming as flame,
coming as voices to teach.

Over the crowd that had gathered outside
a power stirred in the air.

Some people scoffed, but some did believe
as they heard the good news declared.

Three thousand new believers that day
were baptized, believing in Christ.

Dead, then alive, now reigning with God,
Christ was giving new life.

Away from their old lives, freed from their sins,
many joined the disciples in faith.

Yet even more believed day by day,
even down to this time and this place.

Karyl J. Leslie

Summer with God

Summer is a perfect time,
A perfect time of year,
To praise our glorious God above
For every bit of cheer
That we have found in this dear life
And to thank God, too,
For all the times that we've been sad
That God has seen us through.

But many shun the sacred church
In this perfect time of year
And only words of fishing or of
Sleeping late we hear.
"It's vacation time. We won't be home."
Don't leave God in the lurch.
Even away on vacation,
You can grace another church.

Don't leave pews empty, for God's praise
Deserves our strongest voice.
God loves it when God's children meet
And sing and pray. Rejoice!
Bring your cares to God and meet
With other people, who
Will pray with you and for you and
Will help to see you through.

"I pray my best when I'm alone,"
Is what you might hear said,
But God uses many, many hands
To provide your daily bread.
It's not only alone or together
That we worship, pray, and sing.
It's both we need to do, says God,
Who creates each living thing.

God wants to know us each as one,
Each a unique human being,
But God on purpose placed us in
One larger family, seeing
That we each need one another
For love, joy, strength, and more;
And in God's family it's designed
That together we adore

The gracious and compassionate God,
Victorious, redeeming Christ,
And holy, insightful Spirit.
Let's gather and add spice
To our lives through worshiping
And hearing God's good word
And then go back into the world
And let good news be heard.

Karyl J. Leslie

Any Sunday Morning

Today is Sunday, and it's clear
That we won't gain by sitting here
All alone at home all day:
To share with others and to pray
Within the fellowship of Christ
Is what will make things turn out right.

God has called us to rejoice
And join with others our own voice
In praising God for all God's done
And for the promise of daily sun.
We know the sun is there to stay
When night turns into glorious day.

We also know when clouds abound
The sun shines brightly all around.
While we can't see its direct rays,
We know it shines beyond the haze;
And even when the night does come,
The sun still shines on others' homes.

We can know this daily fact:
The sun remains out there intact.
Even when we see it not,
We know it shines out from its spot
In the heavens God has made,
Who gives us light and gives us shade.

And if we know and trust this fact,
We can trust our God to act
Even when we do not feel
God's presence with us is quite real.
God is greater than the sun
And will not leave when day is done.

And so on Sundays we are called
To meet God in some hallowed halls,
To sing with others of God's name,
God's deeds of power to proclaim;
For we are not abandoned here
Without a love to give us cheer.

"Praise to God, eternal praise,"
Let us sing throughout our days
And on Sundays gather round
With others on some hallowed ground.
It is to God we owe this thrust
For God has called both them and us

To meet together once a week
And of God's faithful presence speak,
To sing and praise, to pray and think,
To hear the scriptures read to each.
We are led in worship there
By one who formed it with much prayer.

Food for thought and food for soul
Food to make the broken whole,
Is what we share when we're around
Others where this grace is found;
And there are those within our doors
Who have come to know there's more

For us than just what earth provides.
They need some help to crest the tides
Of life which often fall and rise
And make our lives a bumpy ride.
Happy, sad, reluctant, too;
One who's quarreled may be you

And as you seek God's mercy seat
In a special way each week,
As others come inside the door,
We can see that there's much more
To life than just what we perceive.
We join with others who believe

And some who doubt and some who snore,
But God's life with us is not a bore.
There's majesty and mercy great
Always there for those who wait
Upon our God and trust God's Word,
Which can often be well heard

As others speak of what God's done
In their lives to lift their glum
Feelings and expressions so
To God they know they'll always go,
Because God has the word of life
Which unites in spite of strife.

So let us gather one and all
In whatever hallowed hall
Is for us our spiritual home
As we through this life now roam.
There are others on the way
Who can help us watch and pray

Through any dark night of the soul.
God's reach through them can make us whole.
God has not left us on our own;
God has not left us all alone.
Instead God gives throughout our lives
Others whose hopes with ours rise

To God's love and glory fine
'Til we reach end of the line
And enter then our heavenly home
No more to wander or to roam.
God gives us hope. God gives us life
When we follow Christ, who died

And rose again so we would know
God's power and love do overflow.
Today is Sunday, and it's clear
That no one gains by sitting there
All alone at home all day.
So meet with us and humbly pray

That God to you might be better known
As we gather about God's throne.
God wants you to know truly
That God provides the victory
Of good over evil, life over death,
Love over hate, and infinite wealth

Of what really matters for those who heed
God's offer that they might be freed
From the tyranny that breaks up hearts
Whenever any try to start
To live for themselves alone.
It is not thus that God is known.

But God has called each one – Yes, you –
To show God's love for others who
May be struggling with life's ills
Or with the devil's scheming chills
That freeze us so we cannot move
In God's holy way of love.

So let's be touched and touch one more
Of those who come within the door
Of our favorite worship spot.
Let us share God's love a lot.
And may it be that outside, too,
We show the world what God can do

With our lives, though broken by
Things we never should have tried.
Sins forgiven, hearts are cleansed.
Toward God our souls are bent.
On this Sunday let us go
To the church and God's love show.

A Timid Old Man

There once was a man,
A timid old man,
Who spoke, oh, so softly,
And touched, oh, so lightly.

But speak he did.
He touched many, too.
His love came from God
And poured timidly through;

And the people all knew
When they saw that old man
What warmth there could be
In the touch of a hand.

Simple Prayer

I talk to God. "Dear God," I say,
"Thank you for the loving way
You receive each prayer I pray
And invite me every day
To pause and talk to you a while.
When I do, it makes me smile.

"I talk to you. It helps me know
That you are with me while I grow;
And every day, it is the same:
I am always glad I came
To talk to you and listen, too,
To find what you want me to do."

On Arising

Dear God, Please guide me through this day
In what I think and do and say.
Please keep me always in your way
That I might not go far astray.
This is what I humbly pray
As I start this brand new day.

Patience

My CD's, their music,
My radio's songs,
Can help so much
To soothe many wrongs.

To relax and just listen
While someone else sings
Of the pain and the joy
Each day seems to bring

Puts things in balance,
Perspective, they say,
And I know once again
It's just one more day,

A day with its downs,
But be patient and wait,
In time there'll be ups
Which will even the slate.

God takes care
And puts balance in things:
Have there been any winters
Not followed by springs?

My Prayer

Father God, be with me, guide me,
Please keep watch whate'er betide me.
On my strength alone I can't go,
But with you I can, I know.

Mother God, be ever near me.
May your love forever cheer me.
When I see another hurting
May I never be deserting.

Karyl J. Leslie

Where Has the Lord Gone?

Where has the Lord gone?
I cannot find Him.

Look to your right,
Look to your left;
Look in front,
Look in back;
Look up above,
Look down below;
God is there.
God is here.

Praise the Lord!

Breezes

The breeze outside is nice today.
It makes me want to stay and play
Out in the sunshine bright and clear,
But there is lots to do in here.

I think I'll go outside a while,
Because fresh air will make me smile,
And then with gladness in my heart
My indoor tasks I will then start.

Karyl J. Leslie

A Parting Prayer

The time has come to say goodbye,
As Pastor, anyway.
But that does not mean that I will
Cease for you to pray.

In every church that I have served
I've come to love you all,
Even if sometimes we didn't
See eye to eye at all.

You have become so dear to me
In the times we've had;
And keeping you in my heart
Will often make me glad.

Sometimes we've found ourselves to be
Mad, bad, or sad, or glad;
But let's hold on to all good things
That God has let us have.

We go to new adventures.
Sometimes our paths will cross,
But that does not mean certainly
We won't feel any loss.

For change is hard; but change is good.
We grow through changing times;
And now I ask for blessings
Upon your lives and mine.

As we find our way anew
And answer God's new call,
May we remember always
That Christ is Lord of all;

Goodbye is not forever;
In heaven we'll meet again;
And we will always in Christ's name
Know love that never ends.

Peace and love and blessings
I pray for you this day,
And in God's saving grace I pray
That you will always stay.

July Readings

It's About Time

July is the seventh month.
It comes this time each year.
Do you enjoy the summer
With its skies both blue and clear?

When July rolls around each year,
The year becomes half through.
Have you made good on half the things
You first set out to do?

It's not too late to start now
If you have had a dream
Of what you would accomplish
In the bright new year's gleam.

Today is not too soon to start.
Tomorrow is too late
To begin your life, with God,
To work to re-create.

Did you want to lose some weight,
Start exercising, too?
Is there in you a habit
You want to quit anew?

If you once had a vision
Of what you would like to be,
Don't delay. Begin right now
Your new future to see.

It's not too late. Start over
Your new year's hopes and dreams
To contemplate, and soon begin
To improve what each day means.

There's half a year remaining
In which you can decide
To make some progress every day
And not just run and hide

From the things you need to do
To make large or small strides
Into a future filled with hope
Because with God you've tried

To do what God has called you to,
To be a you you like.
Look it over and begin
To take that noble hike

Into a future where you can
Be proud of who you are,
And celebrate that you've begun
Something you've put off far

Too long already in your life.
Take a look around.
Pick up your head, keep your eyes
From viewing just the ground.

You can do it, yes, you can.
It's been done before.
Just follow God's direction
And open that new door

That God has placed before you
To fill you up with hope.
Take a step; go through it now.
Don't just stand and mope

That you have not yet become
As perfect as you want.
Perfection isn't quite as great
As humility of heart.

We need to keep you humble,
So we won't let you be
Perfect in this lifetime.
It's in the next you'll see

Perfection all around you.
It's not promised here on earth.
God says, just do what you can
With every day's new birth.

With God's help you'll find out
That each day you can live
Surrounded by forgiveness
And the grace God freely gives.

So don't worry about failure.
Just try and try again.
Get up each time you fall down,
And you will always win.

Perfection is just not the goal.
There's only One who is;
And that One is the only One
Who can fill your life with bliss.

Karyl J. Leslie

Hope

In a time of fear and madness,
In a world so full of badness,
It helps my heart to know
Somewhere some love can grow,
Because God knows and cares
How much each one can bear.

Ready for the Day

It's morning, and I'm wide awake,
Ready the day's tasks to take
And try to fulfill and accomplish them.
I'll find I have succeeded when
I've caught up on important things
And looked with blessing on what day brings.

KARYL J. LESLIE

Good Morning, Good Day

Good morning to you.
The day starts anew.
The skies may be cloudy,
But God's love shines brightly;
And that is the way
We start every day.

Good morning to you.
My small prayer for you
Is that you know God's love
And your day is full of
God's blessings and grace
Through all the day's race.

Good morning to you.
I hope through and through
Your day and encounters
You'll find small reminders
That you have been called
By God for the world.

Good morning to you.
The gifts that you use
Spread God's love around you
So it may be found you
Have blessed the whole world
Through the seeds you have hurled

On good soil and bad,
On places that had
Birds or thorns come up
And try growth to choke out.
It may be your seed
Will fill someone's need.

So smile at all people.
Remember the steeple
That points us toward God
And infinite love.
May God's blessings fill you
And hate never chill you.

Good morning to you.
Good afternoon, too.
And as evening comes up
May God fill your cup up
With mercy and grace
And rest as you place

Your life in God's hands
And know that what's grand
Awaits you in heaven
After you've given
Your heart to the Christ
And followed Christ's life.

Karyl J. Leslie

New Eyes

I wonder what I'd see if I
Looked at things with brand new eyes,
Eyes which made the darkness light
And looked with hope upon my plight.

I'd like to have the eyes that see
How much of life is mystery
Given by God in heaven above,
Given by God of steadfast love.

What if, wherever I looked, I'd see
Hope streaming ahead of me?
What if I saw with eyes of love
God still reigns in heaven above?

The bad is never here to stay.
All looks fine in light of day.
It's darkest before the dawn, they say,
So hold on for your glorious day,

A day when God will rain on you,
Not water, but many blessings true;
For God can take the darkest night
And make its shadows take their flight.

And the Lord...

And the Lord looked down on him and said,
"Let there be Light."
And the man opened his eyes and saw the light,
but it was bright so that it hurt.
So the man closed his eyes because the
brightness of the light hurt them.
And to this very day he lives in darkness.

And the Lord looked down on him and said,
"Lift up your thoughts."
And the man in the ditch tried,
but he could not get his thoughts above his own level
Because all he could see and think about
were the four walls enclosing him in the hole.
And there he has remained.

And the Lord looked down on him and felt a
deep compassion.
And He said to the troubled man,
"My friend, I can see you are troubled.
Look up and accept my peace."
And the man looked up into His face and saw
the love that was there.
As he looked, he more and more felt not only
a deep sense of peace and relief,
but also a real joy began creeping into his soul.

And the man got up and walked,
never taking his eyes from his Lord.
And when he fell,
the One who had called him "friend"
turned and came back from His leading position
to help him back to his feet.

And as the man followed,
his falls became less and less frequent,
and he lived,
and he loved,
and he learned,
and he became.

The Holy One

The Holy One looked upon her and said, "Let there be Light"
And the woman opened her eyes and saw the light,
but it was bright so that it hurt.
So the woman closed her eyes because the
brightness of the light hurt them.
And to this day she has not dared to open them again.

And the Holy One looked upon her and said,
"Look deeper still. You will find the way through."
And the woman who was buried so deep tried,
but she could not turn her thoughts from her present level,
Because all she could see and think about
were the barriers and weights holding her down.
So there she has remained.

And the Holy One looked upon her with a deep compassion.
And She said to the crippled woman,
"My sister, I can see you are crippled.
Look at me. Accept my peace and my power."

And the woman looked into Her face and saw
the love that was there.
As she looked, she more and more felt
not only a deep sense of peace and relief,
but also a real joy, and power,
began creeping into her soul.

And the woman began to walk,
never taking her heart from her Guide.
And when she fell,
the One who had called her "sister"
turned with Her power, Her life, Her vision,
to help her back to her feet.

And as the woman walked,
her falls became less and less frequent,
and she lived,
and she loved,
and she learned,
and she BECAME!

Time to Dream

Peaceful, quiet.
Now it seems
I have some time
To dream my dreams,

Dreams which make
My life much more
Than something which
I just endure.

We all need dreams
To make our lives
Meaningful
As days go by.

And so I love
To have some time,
To have some quiet,
In which my mind

Can dream its dreams
And plan its plans,
Hope its hopes,
And know I can

With help from God
Be free to try
Whether I fail
Or learn to fly!

Karyl J. Leslie

Singing Praise

May we, like Paul and Silas,
Sing when our times seem bad.
May we sing loud or quiet
'Til our hearts become glad.

May we praise God in heaven.
May we praise God within.
May we praise God, who loves us,
As new life we begin.

May blessings be upon us
As we go forth from here,
And may we be a blessing
To all whom we come near.

Blue Sky

The sky is blue,
The sun is high.
Whoop-de-do,
And My-oh-my.

Psalm 19, rephrased

I do declare, say the heavens,
That God is great, say the skies,
From the evening, adds the earth,
To the morning's bright sunrise.

The sun journeys, says the wildlife,
Like a bridegroom going forth;
Dressed in splendor, say the rivers,
Joyously running each day's course.

God Almighty, say the humans,
Has a Law which is divine,
Guiding us each day in glory
To the end of space and time.

Hallelujah to the Only
Holy God, who lives on high.
Keep me from sin's vast dominion.
Save me so that I won't die.

May the One who shows such great love
Bless the thoughts that fill our minds,
When we try like God the Holy
One to live in light sublime.

Trusting God in Difficult Times

Good news did not come today.
Instead, there's one for whom to pray,
For trouble's come unto this one,
Which may be hard before it's done.

News she didn't want to hear
Is what came calling at her ear.
How to cope? How to abide
With something it's no good to hide?

The doctor said, "There's room for hope,"
But in the meantime, how to cope
Is the question that presses in
And makes the joy seem awfully thin.

What choices to make, what hope to have?
For wounded souls, is there a salve
That can make things brighter seem
Even when it all feels like a dream —

A bad dream from which you'd like to awake?
What is the path that you should take?
It will be difficult for a while,
But when you can, maybe you'll smile,

Because although the news sounds grim
You believe in God and trust God then
Not to abandon you or forsake
You when your soul begins to quake.

Facing the unknown as you must,
Can you find it in you your God to trust?
That doesn't mean it won't ever be hard
Or that you've been dealt a very fair card.

No, it's not fair. No, not at all.
Why did this upon you fall?
There may be no rhyme or reason to say
Why you received this news today;

But maybe still God has something good
To come out of this however it would
Come to you at the end of the day.
Do you trust God when you try to pray?

Sometimes maybe some doubts arise
And tears well up in both your eyes,
But tears are healthy to be shed,
And through them you might be led

To put your hope in God and those
That work with you, the ones God chose
To give you a hand, to help see you through
All this stuff that for you is so new.

You do not have to walk alone,
For others are coming before God's throne
To intercede on your behalf.
Once in a while may they make you laugh.

Laughter and tears, and trust and fears,
Will be with you sometimes very near,
But live with hope in God above,
Who holds you forever in divine love.

Nothing can happen to you that God
Doesn't see or care about. Isn't it odd
That God would think so much of you,
To be with you every step through

This challenge of life? May you succeed
In trusting God for your every need.
Trust in the people God sends to help you
And rely on them to help you through.

You may feel you're all alone,
But to God you are God's very own
Precious child God won't desert
No matter how badly you may hurt.

So sometimes look beyond the skies;
Try to open your very eyes
To see the good God's planned for you,
And trust in God to see you through.

Poetry

My poetry is for me a release
From worries and pressures that don't seem to cease.
In writing it out I sometimes will find
Answers that come by the end of a line.

Maybe it's changing my thoughts in a way
Trying to rhyme the words that I say.
I still think about the problem at hand,
But getting it out does help me to stand.

It's a pressure release that helps me to see
There's always a chance for me to get free
And live life again in a new sort of way
Free from that problem the rest of the day.

Condolences, Part 1

Now the day is over.
The funeral's passed by.
Today's a new beginning
Even though we sigh.

Our loved one's not among us
In human shape or form;
While inside our minds and hearts
It sometimes seems to storm.

Memories come crashing
Into our purview.
They distract or cheer us
As we begin anew.

Our loved one is gone from us,
Out of sight, not mind,
And it seems as we go on
New sadnesses we find.

Yet on the other hand, there
Are memories just so good
That we smile with warmth and joy,
So full of gratitude

For the times we've shared with
Our loved one on the earth,
Our loved one who's gone on to
A new and joyous birth

Into God's great kingdom
Where the sounds arise
Day and night to shower
God with joyous praise.

For all is now victorious.
They are now at rest
From their earthly labors.
Every moment's blessed

With a fresh awareness
Of the glory that God has.
It lights their way, it lights their play
As day to day they pass

With the holy angels,
God's heavenly host of song,
And now with refreshed voices
They can sing along.

Oh, the sound is glorious
Of all their singing hearts,
With praise flowing from even
Prior hidden parts.

The beauty there is awesome.
God's glory shines all 'round
And with all creatures praising,
How glorious is the sound.

So we don't need to worry
About our loved one hence
Because he or she's arrived now
Beyond the gilded fence

That marks the home that God's made
For God's beloved ones;
And when your place is ready,
Jesus says, "Now come."

"Come and taste the banquet.
Come, be filled with joy.
Come, drink living water.
Each new day's like a toy

Which you can unwrap gaily
As in heaven you live."
Never in your wildest
Dreams did you perceive

What you'll then be seeing,
The wondrous sounds you'll hear.
You've never seen so clearly
Or heard with such good cheer.

So while with sadness we grieve
And wish our loved ones here,
We take comfort that they've
Entered all the cheer

That awaits in heaven
When this life is past
And our home on the earth here
Is set behind at last.

Karyl J. Leslie

Condolences, Part 2

Now the day is over.
The funeral's passed by.
Today's a new beginning
Even though you sigh.

Your loved one's not among us
In human shape or form.
But has gone on to glory
And suffers no more harm.

You one day will join them
At God's beloved shore
And then it will be your turn
To sing with praise and more.

Your days on earth are over.
Your funeral's passed by.
You have a new beginning
Even though you sigh

With love for those you've left
Behind upon the earth
So now you pray intently
For each soul's holy birth

Into the realm of God's love,
A realm that never ends,
That carries us ever forward
With loving, blessed friends,

Friends on earth, in heaven,
And through eternity,
All rejoicing in Christ
And in the victory

That's been won for all time,
In spite of skirmishes
With the evil forces
That we have no wish

To give our allegiance
Or our loyalty.
We'd rather stick with the One
Who truly holds the key

To the heavenly portals
Where one day, we, too,
Will enter with all gladness
When this life is through.

Regrets we won't remember.
Grudges fall away.
When we, too, enter glory,
What a lovely day

Is in store for us who
Believe Christ's living word
And take him at his promise.
Our deepest prayers were heard.

So while with sadness we grieve
And wish our loved ones here,
We take comfort that they've
Entered all the cheer

That awaits in heaven
When this life is past
And our home on earth here
Is set behind at last.

Each day will be a new one
With challenges and tasks,
But keep the faith, hold on now,
And do whate'er God asks

So you also can come home
At the end of earthly days
And hear God's priceless voice
Speak to you and say,

"Well done, my faithful servant.
You have done my will.
Welcome home with gladness."
Let your heart be still

If only for a moment.
Pause and let sink in
The wonder of the victory
Over death and sin

That Christ has won for all who
Seek to follow him,
Who trust him for salvation
And seek his way to live.

August Readings

Answered Prayer

I talk to God. "Dear God," I say,
"I'm glad to come to you and pray.
I tell you what is on my mind;
And when I do I always find
That you are surely waiting there
To hear and answer every prayer.

"Sometimes you answer and say yes
To what has been my main request.
Sometimes, instead, you make me wait
For something that will be just great.
At other times you may say no
To something that won't help me grow.

"I need to trust you all the while
That you would like to see me smile.
I know that sometimes what I ask
Is not a good thing that will last.
You only want what's best for me.
That is what I try to see.

"But I can tell you anything,
And I can tell you everything
That I think or feel each day.
It's such a simple way to pray
And helps me love you more each day,
So I'll take the time to pray."

KARYL J. LESLIE

Patterns of Prayer

I never know quite what I'll say
When I sit down just to pray.
Writing is one way I find
To open up my heart and mind;

And as I write, "Dear God," I find
Thoughts and feelings come to mind,
So I write down whatever's there
And take it right to God in prayer.

At other times, there are no words,
But even so my prayer is heard
By God, who knows what's in my heart
Because great God is mighty smart.

So even if I'm coloring,
God knows just what each color means
In the great grand scheme of things
And what each note means when I sing.

Sometimes I just sit quietly
And let my body's breathing be
A sign of God's infinity
And of God's daily care for me.

So if I have no words to say
It doesn't mean I cannot pray,
For God knows every thought of mine.
I merely need to give some time

To thinking of how God is near
And speaks in every sound I hear
And comes in every breath I take.
God is Love. Make no mistake.

God Is Good

Celebrate the gift of life,
Whatever shape your life is in.
God is good, gracious, and true.
God declares great love for you.

No matter what your circumstance,
No matter what is in your glance,
No matter whether good or bad,
No matter, be it happy or sad,

God in all things works for good.
Let it be rightly understood
That even if God brings us rain,
God brings rainbows through the pain.

In whatever circumstance
You find yourself, let your glance
Fall on the good God works in it,
Not just beside, but in the midst.

Even while events still flow,
May you in your deep heart know
That God is with you all the way
Even if you neglect to pray.

Don't mistake: God loves to hear
Your prayers and thanks and heartfelt pleas,
But God does not depend on these
In order to meet all your needs.

God knows your needs before you do.
God knows your wants and "druthers," too.
God knows what's best of all to do.
Trust in God to see you through –

Maybe not the way you thought,
Maybe not how you think God ought,
But in the ways that are best for you
And all the world for eternity through.

God will not fail or abandon you.
It may be beyond what you ever knew,
But trust the love of Jesus Christ,
In whom God came to give you Life.

One and one and one and three,
God blesses us abundantly.
Would we open up our eyes,
We'd see each day a nice surprise.

So I invite you, one and all,
To join me in a journey call,
To turn to God again, anew,
And see what great things God will do.

Sweet Slumber

Toward the end of day today
I get ready down to lay
My body so to give it rest
And pray tonight my sleep is blest.

Choices

I did a task this morning
That I wanted to complete.
It was on my to-do list
And I didn't want to miss.

I put a check mark on my list
To show I had accomplished this.
One more check upon the page
Of things to do on this day's stage.

Now on to another task.
Maybe later I'll relax
And read or rest, lie down or play,
Maybe take more time to pray.

I thank you, God, for this great day
Even if at times I say,
"I do not know what I should do
With all this time that's come from you."

Does it matter in the end
How I choose this day to spend?
"Yes and no" comes to my mind.
Hopefully I'll even find

That what I do and what I choose
May be a blessing God can use,
Not only for myself alone,
But also for another soul.

Blessings

God, blessings from you pour on us,
And most abundantly.
You show your love in many ways.
Help us to thankful be:

For all the things you give to us,
For people in our lives,
For growing grass and tall oak trees,
Which help our spirits thrive.

We thank you most for Jesus Christ,
Who died that we may live.
It's hard for us to understand
The great love he did give.

We thank you that he lives again
And gives us life anew.
We thank you that he's with us now
Through us his work to do:

To be his eyes, his ears, his arms
That we might others reach;
To be his mouth with words of love
Which should be all our speech.

Through us his feet go to and fro;
They walk the city streets;
They walk along the country roads,
With love the folk to greet.

To share Christ's love and bounty thus
Is a special gift God gave
To us that we may reach out now
And bring to Christ to save

All who would come and thankful be
For life redeemed with God
And for our bread, and for our care,
Our love, and earthen sod.

For all of God's creation thus,
May we, too, be well pleased,
And use what we've been given here
That others' needs be eased.

God gave us blessings far and wide,
Beyond what we deserved.
God gives us blessings every day
That others might be served.

Be thankful, then, for blessings kind
Of every sort and ilk,
And in thanksgiving to our God
Give life and hope and milk.

The "milk of human kindness," though,
Will not fill all the need.
Real milk and bread we must share, too,
If God's call we will heed.

With thanks let's share our daily bread
With others God holds dear
Whether they are quite far away
Or maybe yet right here.

For there are many needs to fill
And we must do our part
While not forgetting all the needs
Of the human heart.

Christ is our joy and is our peace.
May Christ come shining through
Every little and great thing
We think or say or do.

We're blessed to be a blessing now,
Not waiting 'til we're full.
We're blessed to be a blessing here
And grow much more thankful.

With kindness in the name of Christ,
Each loving act we do
Because of our great thankfulness
To you, yes, God, to you.

God, bless us as we think of you
And of the world's great need.
God, bless us as we learn to share.
God, bless every good deed.

Your Story

Tell us your story; tell it so true,
Tell us your story, how God has touched you.
How have you seen the blessings of God?
Where does God lead you, how does God prod
You to do what is loving, gracious, and free?
Tell it to us, so we, too, can see

God in the midst of everyday life,
Where God can touch us, how can the light
Of God become clear as we live every day?
Tell us your story, show us the way
You open yourself to the power of Christ.
Help us to know in a way that is right

How God has touched you and how, like you,
We can know that we've been touched, too.
God's Spirit is present in each of our lives,
In the midst of the good, in the midst of the strife.
God never leaves us alone to ourselves.
Let us worship and share and give of our help.

New Beginnings

It's August now. School's soon to start.
The summer's gone by fast.
Soon it's off to school again.
Vacation doesn't last.

But we'll be glad as we go back
To see new friends and old,
To learn new things and grow new dreams
As the year unfolds.

The most important lessons, though,
Are those we learn at church.
Why, then, when it is time to go
Do we start to lurch

Away and say, why bother
To go to Sunday School
Or to Sunday worship?
We're busy, as a rule.

How should we live? How should we give
To people near and far,
Our hearts, our love, and our respect?
Let's leave the door ajar,

The door of heart and mind and soul,
The door of living ways.
Let's live as God wants us to live.
It truly, truly pays.

Parts of our world are in a mess.
They're in a mess, we see.
How better can we sort out
Than by God's priorities?

We try, we try, we conquer.
We try, we try, we fail.
But we are loved by God above,
Whose mercies never pale.

Let's hear it for life! Let's not fear death
Or any earthly thing,
For God has promised those who trust
They can let their hearts take wing.

If we study in God's Word
And talk and sing and pray,
Our lives can have great meaning
And nothing to throw away.

So, Hooray for God, for Jesus Christ,
The Holy Spirit, too.
The Three-in-One and One-in-Three
Can our lives renew.

Let's gather once more at the church's door.
Come in, come in, please do;
For you are valued very much
No matter what you do.

"Just as I am, without one plea,"
We turn to God and say,
And put our hands in God's own hand
To walk along the way,

The way that leads to all good things
And wonders ever new.
Come join us as we pursue
The things that are truly true.

New beginnings for some of us,
Renewal for others we see.
Let's love God truly now
And see what we can be;

For we can be more than we are.
God's love can see us through.
So come and join us Sundays
And share Good News that's true.

Karyl J. Leslie

Joyful Kindness ABC

A
Blessed
Consequence
Does
Exist,
For
God
Has
In
Joyful
Kindness
Loved
Many
Nations
Of
People,
Quoting
Redemption,
Salvation,
Toward
Unfortunate
Victims
Whom
(X) Christ
Yet
Zealously forgives.

("X" represents the Greek letter for the "Ch" of "Christ.")

A Better Chance ABC

A
Better
Chance
Does
Exist,
For
Grace
Has
Imparted
Justice,
Kindness,
Love,
Meaning.
Now
Open
Precise
Queries
Right.
Starting
Today,
Uselessness,
Vanity,
Will
eXit
Your
Zealousness.

Karyl J. Leslie

The Open Door ABC

As we live our lives today,
Blindness needn't have a say,
Causing us to miss the grace
Daily God puts into place.
Everyone is precious here
For Christ has died to give us cheer.
God has opened heaven's door
Holding it 'til more and more
Impacted people come right in
Joyfully remembering,
Keeping in their heart's awareness
Lovingkindness, graciousness
Manifested forth by God.
Now we know salvation's prod
Opening to us a new life
Praising God even in strife,
Questioning not God's love divine.
Rightly may God's light forth shine,
Sending love and righteousness
To a world that knows distress.
Up from the dead did Christ arise,
Very life and love's surprise,
Wanting for us paradise.
eXamine now your heart's reprise.
You are now invited in.
Zestfully with Christ begin.

Dedication

I will write this poem now
As I take the time to bow
Both my head and heart before
The One who knows all that's in store
For me before the day is done.
I pray the vict'ry will be won
Today both over sloth and sleep
While my appointed tasks I keep.

Nighttime Rest

It's getting kind of late.
I'm feeling kind of tired.
In spite of getting not much done
I've spent my daily hours.

And soon it's time to go to bed.
I hope I fall asleep;
And if I sleep, I pray that I
Will have some sacred hours,

Hours when I just lie and rest
In God's great loving care
And trust that God will bring the best
Of healing balm God pours.

Oh, to sleep a peaceful sleep
That it may healing bring;
But if I find I am awake,
I pray God's blessing then.

An Important Lesson

It's hard to believe it's the end of the month.
The weeks have gone by so fast.
Tomorrow begins another month.
Summer is almost past.

For many I know, school will begin
Tomorrow. They're likely to burst.
I hope that they will find they've got
A special kind of thirst:

A thirst for knowledge and for growth,
A thirst to stretch their minds;
And throughout the whole school year,
I hope they joy will find

In meeting others and helping them,
In learning thus to know
That together with others it shall be
A better way to go

Than to try to live life all alone
And never reach out of ourselves.
God's put us here together so
We can all help and be helped.

So as the school year soon begins
Let's strive to learn this fact,
That putting us here together like this
Was one of God's finest acts.

September Readings

Changes

Autumn is drawing closer.
Some days the air is cool.
We get out sweaters and jackets
For the kids to wear to school.

But then the air gets warmer
As the day continues on,
And once upon a little while
There comes the threat of storm.

We carry our umbrellas
To work or to the mall.
We try to be prepared
For any coming squall.

Life is like the autumn.
Sometimes it's crisp and cool,
But then we must prepare for change
So we don't play the fool.

Change in seasons, change in days,
Change is all around.
Hopefully we'll adapt
And keep our thinking sound.

Everyone, Back to School!

Back to school now. Let us say,
"May we all enroll today.
Whether young or whether old,
Or in between, let us be bold

Enough to say, 'There's more to learn.'
Let us hunger, let us yearn
For knowledge and for wisdom, too."
That is very good to do.

Young or old, we never know
All there is God wants to show
Us about God's holy Word
Or even things about this world.

Relationships. Can you improve
The ones God's given for your good?
And can you even, with help, try
To release those with whom you fight

For greater honor or respect?
If you try, can you reflect
On what in them can be for good?
Can they be better understood?

Of course they can, and so can you.
We can learn each other to
Understand better than we do
And learn that it is always true

That we have some things to share
If we don't try to compare
One as better, one as worse.
Because God's world is so diverse

We can find good about each
Person or each thing we see,
For God works in all things for good.
With faith in God, that's understood;

But sometimes it is very hard
To find the things God does that are
For our good, though we complain.
Complaining is just always vain.

We can share hopes, dreams, and thoughts
About the good and bad that's brought
Us to our knees in grief profound
Or lifted us in relief's sound.

So let us all go back to school
So we can live the Golden Rule
Better than we have before
And live the love God has in store

For us and for all those we meet.
In each one is something sweet.
Even though the smell is rank,
Every person we can thank

For something good that God has wrought
In their lives and to us brought
The chance to meet the Christ in them,
Richer, poorer, fat, or thin.

Back to school now. Let each say,
"Yes, I will enroll today.
No matter whether young or old,
I will dare to be so bold

As to admit I know not all
The wisdom God gives to stand tall
As in life I proceed on
And live more like Christ, God the Son."

Thank you, God, for all your gifts,
For those who teach and those who lift
Our people young and people old
To lives that shine with purer gold,

As you refine us, precious each.
Help us more your love to seek
And to express through our whole lives.
That is such a blessed prize.

May we read and may we seek
Through others with whom we may speak
To learn much more of your own ways
And to improve throughout our days.

Even if our hairs are gray,
Or we have none in the way,
Let us find in you our best;
And may all students be quite blessed.

Sunday Morning

Hello, Hello. It's Sunday morning.
We're all dressed and ready to go
Off to church to worship with others,
Off to church God's Word to know.
But what will we find when we get there?
Empty seats row after row?

Where are you this Sunday morning,
This fine little resurrection day?
Are you home or are you golfing?
Have you decided to stay away?
We sure miss you when you're not here.
That is what I want to say.

Without you, our worship is lamer.
Without you, our songs aren't as strong.
Without you, there are holes in our spirit,
And we feel that something is wrong.
Without you, God's praise is weaker,
So why don't you now come along?

Karyl J. Leslie

Your Part

I've been dreaming recently
I'm working in a church,
A very busy, active one
In which I tend to lurch

Into this and that. It seems
I'm busy all the time;
But in my dreams things don't always
Turn out to be fine.

There's stress and strain, but joy there, too.
I find joy in my work.
But sometimes in doing one thing,
There's something else I shirk.

That's why it's not one person's job
To do whatever's needed.
It takes a lot of people's gifts
To show that God is heeded

And that we seek to do God's will
And not merely our own.
We must all work together
To make church a happy home –

A place where people gather
Without judgment or fights
Because we follow Jesus,
Who is the Light of Lights.

You have a gift God gave you
To put into the work.
God has a job designed for you
To help the Spirit perk,

The Spirit of the love of God
Shown through human ones,
Which welcomes all to God's embrace,
Inviting all to come.

And so you're needed. Yes, you are.
You alone can do
The job, the task, the ministry
God set aside for you.

A church has many members
Just as the body does,
And each one has a special role
To fulfill because

That's the way God set it up.
You're special, don't you know?
Without the gift you offer,
The church cannot quite grow

To be what God intends it
In your own place and time.
So you're required to use your gifts
To make the whole refined.

A gift in you, a gift in me,
A gift in him and her —
And all are needed, for it's God
Who did each gift confer

For the good that benefits
Not the church alone
But all the people God would call
Through you to "come on home."

So reach out in God's Spirit,
With God's own loving heart,
And though you don't feel worthy,
With others take your part

To do whatever you can
To reach out in God's name
And make each guest and visitor
Be very glad they came.

Refine your gifts, and build each one
As strong and straight and true
As is possible when God
Works God's will in you.

May Your Skies Be Blue

May blue skies be abundant
Even when the clouds are gray.
May you trust in God's great wisdom
As you go along your way.
Even when it's not apparent,
It is there to guide you on.
May you live a life of meaning
Led by God's own holy song.

A Long, Long Day

It's been a long and tiring day.
At least it started out that way
And I was tired from the start.
It was hard to put my heart
Into anything I did
Because I was feeling so fatigued.

But now my energy's revived.
I think that I might well survive
The rest of the day that lies before
Me before I close the door
Of my eyes and go to sleep
And "pray the Lord my soul to keep."

Gifts to One Another

As we go through life we have
Tasks to do each day,
Responsibilities to fill
As we travel life's highway.

Some things we must do on our own,
But so much can be shared;
And as we share the times of life
We'll know someone has cared –

Someone has cared not just on earth,
But heavenly beings, too;
And God, above all hopes and prayers,
Just loves to see you through.

For you are God's creation great,
Though you might feel quite low.
God has made you specially.
I want you that to know,

To know and hold tight in your heart
No matter what you think,
For the heart that trusts God's love and grace
Can hold back from the brink

Of despair, depression,
Or the brink of suicide.
God loves you so much today
You nothing need to hide;

For God knows all your inmost thoughts,
Though never spoken aloud,
And God can mend your deepest hurts
When there's no one else around.

But sometimes, be it known to you,
That God's work often is
Done by people on the earth,
So sometimes let them in.

And be it also known to you
That sometimes God will use
You yourself as God's own gift
To someone who is blue.

Though you might not believe it,
You are the perfect one
To help someone open up to grace
As God's love to them you show.

You may not know you're doing it,
But you'll be doing fine
If you walk with one another
And let hope through you shine.

Today's Blessing

When you find yourself all hemmed in
By the cares and tasks of life,
When you find yourself quite worried
Or surrounded by tough strife,
May you know that God is with you
Even though God is unseen,
And may you trust God's promises
To be true and not just dreams.

Karyl J. Leslie

Simple Relief

Today I did some coloring
To try to keep from worrying.
I played some music as I chose
Colors to use for every pose.

It did the trick. It did as hoped.
It helped alleviate my mope,
Which I had known a little while.
Now I again will wear a smile.

A New Song

I've finished all my journaling
And so I'm ready now to sing
And lift my voice into the air
Without a bit of sad despair,
For things are looking up for me
And a bright future I do see.
Although I don't know what it holds
It'll be a time to break the molds.

Karyl J. Leslie

Peace

It's quiet.
The silence
Refreshes my mind.

Humble Prayer

I talk to God and humbly say,
"Thank you for the loving way
You respond each time I pray.
You have such a special way
Of showing how you love each one
From dawn of day to setting sun."

Karyl J. Leslie

Miraculous Day

I know, I know, that it will be
A marvelous, wonderful day today,
No matter what the day will hold.
I watch excitedly as it unfolds.

Whatever good or woe might come
In the day, if I leave home
Or in my apartment safely rest,
I make it my aim always to guess

That the day to come will splendid be
For God made lots of souls like me
Who look at life with hope and faith
No matter what else it might take.

To start the day in hopeful mood
Does a person a lot of good.
For who can tell what miracles may
Occur as we walk through a day?

October Readings

Party Time

A party is occurring now
In the head which I have bowed
In tribute and submission to
The God with whom I have to do.

Karyl J. Leslie

Holy Communion

A lovely Sunday morning
Began with sleeping in,
And after I got up and dressed,
To church I headed then.

I had forgotten that today,
First Sunday of the month,
We would receive Communion,
Which we should never shun.

We remember Jesus
As he met that night with his
Disciples for that supper
That was the end of his

Earthly life among us.
The next day he did die,
Hung up for long hours
On the cross, crucified.

But he was raised from death to life,
So we, too, soon might be;
And he is with us daily
If we have eyes to see.

He meets us in his supper
That we share each time
We break the bread and share the cup
That's filled with drink divine.

Jesus is the host himself
At this table spread
With the cup of blessing
And the holy bread.

So take his life and spirit
Into your flesh and find
You come away quite blessed
With renewed heart and mind.

Every time you drink the cup,
Every time you dine,
Remember and give thanks for
These gifts of bread and wine.

The molecules of bread and juice,
The particles they bear,
Become digested gradually
To touch you everywhere.

Into the bloodstream do they go
To feed body and soul.
They're meant to make you newly live
In a way that's whole.

So receive forgiveness.
Receive a change of heart.
Receive the power of Jesus
To make a brand new start.

Be like him in his glory.
Be like him as he says,
"God, forgive them. They don't know
What's even in their heads."

A new life starts for you and me
Not just when we receive
Forgiveness from God's holy love
But when we, too, believe,

That we are to forgive as well
Just as Christ forgives us.
In the prayer Christ taught us,
He says we really must

Forgive as we're forgiven.
Let others free as well.
In doing so, we free ourselves
From the living hell

Of holding grudges against those
Whom we perceive as bad,
Those by whom we've felt hurt,
Who may have made us sad.

But we've been forgiven so much
Words can never say.
Let's follow just as Jesus said:
Make it a brand new day

For ourselves and others
As we let forgiveness reign.
Open up your heart and life
And never be the same.

Autumn Changes

The leaves are changing color,
A sight I love so well,
And in that creativity of God
I love my soul to dwell.

For autumn is a precious time,
With skies so clear and blue.
It has a perfect temperature
For what I want to do.

Sure, some days and nights are hot or cold,
But moderate holds true
For many, if not most of them
As activities I pursue.

The daylight hours grow shorter.
I do not like that much,
But it makes it cozier at home
To sit and read and such.

October is my favorite month
Of all months of the year.
If you've read what I wrote above,
The reasons will be clear.

The leaves once they start falling
Make a crunchy sound
When you step on them as they
Lie scattered on the ground.

So gather them and make big piles.
Jump up and down in them;
But if you do, watch out because
You'll have to rake again.

Autumn Blessings

Autumn comes and with it grain
And precious drops of gentle rain.
May God your life with blessings fill
And guide and guard you safe until
The day comes when Christ gathers in
All who have believed in Him.

May the cool, crisp autumn now
Cause you to pause a while and bow
Before the Artist's awesome throne,
For it is God and God alone
Who can paint with richest hues
The leaves, the trees, the landscapes, too.

As the seasons change and pass
It seems the world is spinning fast
And life goes by at such a pace
That we feel like we're in a race,
A race to nowhere, round and round,
A race where rest cannot be found.

But it is autumn now at last.
Things don't have to go so fast.
Take a moment, or take two,
Just to stop; look around you.
Seasons come and seasons go
But it's important that you know

That God is steady, steadfast, true,
Who colors the world with vibrant hues
But also brown and gray and plain.
The leaves fall gently with the rain.
It's cooler now, and darkness comes
Earlier with the setting sun,

A sun which sets with orange and red,
A sun which goes early to bed,
At least on this side of the earth,
But far away it's giving birth
To another glorious day
In which children will laugh and play.

The world which God created is vast
And when the shadow on us casts,
The sun rises on the other side
And starts the day with glorious pride
In the beauty God puts in all
The seasons, days, and nights, and fall.

God colors the world with such rich hues,
Reds and oranges, and sky blue,
Our amazement need not wane.
No two days are ever the same.
May the autumn's changing scenes
Add some spice to your life's dreams;

And may the many colors of fall
Show you one and show you all
That God can handle anything.
So let us join our hearts and sing
Praise to God who blesses us
No matter how we fume and fuss.

May the fruits that grow on trees
And fruits of the Spirit without fees
Be abundant in your life.
May you have rest from any strife.
Now I close this lengthy rhyme
Wishing you some sacred time,

Time alone in your heart with God,
Time maybe walking on the sod,
Time for prayer and wonder, too.
That is what I wish for you.
Autumn is here but it won't stay.
Try to rejoice a little each day.

(And don't forget each night to pray.)

Autumn Speaks

The trees outside are beautiful;
The leaves with color are so full.
It makes me think of God's great love,
Painting with colors from above.

The trees are touched by God's great brush;
Each leaf receives its special touch.
Again I think how much God cares
For each and every one God bears.

Each one of us is loved so much
God gives us each our special touch.
Through the colored leaves of fall
We see God's tender love for all.

October Extravagance

October leaves go rustle, rustle
As we all just bustle, bustle
To and fro so busily.
Do we take the time to see
The beauty of God's created hues,
Reds and yellows, greens and blues?

Leaves of gold, red, orange too,
Set against a sky of blue
Or as a carpet on the ground
Making a very pleasant sound,
Remind us of God's vast domain.
Unfeeling how can we remain?

Creation's vast parade of time,
Month to month and years just flying
Can pass us by without a thought.
Don't we see what love God's brought
To us each and every day?
God shows it in so many ways.

Take the time to look and see;
Taste and touch with childlike glee;
Feel the air against your skin,
And always let God's warmth come in.
Smell and hear what's new about
Autumn as you laugh and shout.

The changing of the leaves in fall
Are a wonder that God shows to all
Who would see the beauties there
And at life's changes not be scared,
But welcome them as a chance to grow
And stretch on spiritual tippy-toes.

Appreciate your nice warm home
With windows to keep out the storms
And keep you safe inside its walls,
But don't stay in, for God wants us all
To get out and come to church
And praise God's name for all we're worth!

Comfort

A friend of mine was laid to rest
Today in my old town.
At least for those concerned the most,
I bow my head right now.

I pray for strength and courage
And new direction, too.
Without their loved one in their midst
They'll have new things to do.

A brand new way of life may lie
Ahead for those who loved
The one who has passed on to rest
That they had not thought of.

Now that this one has gone ahead
And no longer needs care,
I pray that those still living
Will know that God's still there,

Still there to walk along with them,
Still there to hear their cries,
Still there to bless each day they live,
Still there in whispered sighs.

I pray that God will hold them
Tenderly, secure
In knowing that God's love for them
Is always very sure.

Daily Prayer

Every day I stop and sit
And talk to God a little bit.
I say whatever's on my mind,
And almost every time I find
That I feel better when I do,
No matter what I'm going through.

Thank you, God, for your great love,
Which surrounds me from above
And from below and all around.
It's the best thing that I've found
To help me feel secure and calm.
Your love is such a healing balm.

I love to talk to you each day.
I know you hear each word I say
And listen to each thought that I
Share with you and really try
To answer in the best of ways
To bring me blessings all my days.

Karyl J. Leslie

Peaceful

No pressure now, no goal to meet.
Just to sit here is so sweet.

A New Stage of Life

In this new stage of my life
I need to refine how I live
And to reprioritize
The life that now before me lies.

The past is gone, over and out,
And now it's time to move on from
Things that kept me as I was.
It's time right now to start the buzz

Of thinking who I want to be
As I approach the age I'll be.
I need some focus for my life,
My new life now with much less strife,

At least in terms of workday world.
My leisure time I now have earned.
Yet I want my life to be grand
Walking with God hand in hand.

Retirement, as it's known by most,
An age of possibility,
Is a stage of wanting to be free
To face a vision yet to be.

Possibilities come and go.
I need to find some way to choose
In what I will engage myself
So I won't be left up on a shelf.

Now I think and I pursue
Things I didn't think before.
It is time for me to be
Truly who I'm meant to be.

At this age and at this stage,
Some choices have been made for me:
What my income soon will be
And where I'll find myself living.

I need to become ready now
To toss away a lot of things
That were useful for a while
But now no longer fit my style.

I had choices – lots – to make,
But God already paved the way.
I am so glad that God can see
Things ahead not just for me.

For God can look and God can see
How we fit together here.
Friends and family, new release.
May God's guidance never cease.

Let me put my trust anew
In what I sense God wants me to
Do here in this time of my
Life as days go marching by.

God works in quite mysterious ways.
May I trust this God in all my days;
But sometimes that seems hard for me
Because I cannot always see

The path that God's set out for me.
My open eyes don't always see
A future broad and full of praise,
Release of troubles day to day,

But maybe God asks just one thing:
To take the next step that God brings
That leads me to the purpose God
Has for me from this point on.

One step is all I need to take
To walk along a path that's great
And in creation take my part.
At least one step will make a start,

So I can be of use to God
In interceding for this world,
In bearing fruit, the kind that lasts,
And going home when this life's past.

Karyl J. Leslie

Live in Hope; Build on Dreams

Together walking hand in hand
We spread God's love throughout the land.
We show the people what it means
To live in hope and build on dreams.

Our hearts, with faith in God above,
Must share God's broad, outreaching love.
Even when we've burdens to bear,
The load is made lighter by God's care.

We spread the Word throughout the world
And hope and pray we have been heard.
All people need to know of God.
They need God's love and need God's prod.

So we must do all we can do
To show God's love for every you.
Then all can know how much it means
To live in hope and build on dreams.

Indescribable

At ten this morning I looked up.
I saw a sight so rare.
I can't describe it well at all.
There's nothing to compare.

It wasn't like a this or that
Or any other thing.
I can't even describe it as
A bird with tiny wings.

And so, let your imagining
Dream up what you will.
Imagine what you can't describe.
With awe your spirit fill.

November Readings

A Morning Prayer

In this day's beginning,
Now that night's passed by,
May God guide my actions,
Every prayer I sigh.

May I come to God's will
More than God to mine.
May the present substance
Of me be refined.

Just as gold is purer
When it goes through fire,
So may my life shine forth
As God will desire.

My prayer for today is,
As I journey forth,
May God make this day one
Of infinite fine worth.

In Perfect Harmony?

Sometimes we Christians act as if
We're the smartest ones that live.
We each think we know what's best
And do not pause to give a rest

To the opinions that we have.
We think that others are naïve
And mistaken in their views.
We just don't want to think things new.

Sibling rivalry in the family of God?
Don't you think it kind of odd
That we might live with frowny faces
When we see each other in various places?

Love is the word of God most strong.
In harmony can we sing songs
Of faith, of trust, of hope, of peace,
Of forgiveness, which is, O so sweet?

Can we let ourselves be swayed
To look at each other as God-made
And think that differences make a grand
Feast of variety in the land?

Each of us is needed so,
Without each other we can't go
In the love that God sets forth
To be for us the quite right course.

So let's listen to the wisdom that
God gives each one so it can add
To the perspective that we bring
To mundane and to holy things.

Let's sing our notes, though not the same,
And try in tune to gain our fame
By the way we blend with others
Who are Christian sisters, brothers.

Let's try to live in harmony sweet
Until we sit at Jesus' feet
With those we mightn't expect to see
In heaven's blessed company.

Karyl J. Leslie

The Spice of Life

Last month I wondered how
The foliage would be.
What do you know?
I saw all the colors
On my own front yard tree.

On that one tree I saw at once
Leaves of many hues.
There were red ones and yellow,
Orange and green,
And often the sky was blue.

During fall foliage time,
Driving along I saw
Scenes of beauty that I thought
Were extraordinarily fine.

I love autumn with all its colors.
It shows me that our God must be
A Great Creator, Artist, Host,
An Extravagant
Bestower of Variety.

The beauty of the flowers
And the birds of the air,
The fish in the tank,
The crops that we grow,
And the lives that we share

Are full of various colors,
Shapes, sizes, tastes,
Textures, and smells.
And then there are the wondrous varied tones
Of musical instruments, voices, and bells.

In our times together,
Our differences can
Call and challenge us to grow,
Stretch, love, and learn,
And reach outward and in.

So much variety in
Creation and lives
Can only be given by
One who is wise.

In the Bible, too, there's history
And many tales to be told.
A variety of stories,
Letters, songs, proverbs,
All help to unfold

God's word, work, and will
As they were understood
And known in that day.
Life stories, dreams, sermons,
Miracles, more,
Bring things to light
In a marvelous way.

Karyl J. Leslie

If You Are Lonely

If you are lonely
There's a dark cloud above.
It's so terribly thick
The light can't get through.

You feel so downcast,
You feel so blue,
Your eyes are blind
To the good around you.

You put yourself down,
Think others do, too.
It's awfully depressing,
Just too much for you.

You think no one cares.
Well, just don't give up.
With patience and faith
The sun will come back.

You may want to give up,
But isn't it clear
That the warmth of God's love
Will always be near?

Delighted?

In autumn when the leaves do change
I look with wonder on
The beauty God created as
The year marches along.

The reds and yellows, orange, too,
Amaze my earthly eyes;
And I rejoice to look at
The leaves against blue skies.

The time the leaves are colorful
As they hang upon the tree
I like much better than when they
Fall down dried up like me.

Sometimes I feel bright like a leaf
That beams with color full;
And other times I'm all worn out.
The color becomes dull,

And I begin to feel a bit
Like a lifeless leaf that falls
Only to get crunched under foot
And crumbled up so small.

For sometimes I am sad inside.
I feel no earthly good,
And it begins to feel as though
My heart is made of wood.

It takes a pounding as it lies
Unmoving on the ground.
Oh, how at times like that I'd like
To hear a giggling sound

Rise up with spontaneity
From a little child who plays
And sees delight in everything
And new joys every day.

Am I too old to giggle?
Have I forgotten how?
If I have, it is a skill
I need to reclaim now.

May I see life through a child's eyes
And often delighted be
As when the leaves change color
And show God's artistry.

Precious Variety

How can we see the beauties of God's creation
And not want to give God our praise?

How can we see the colors of the autumn leaves
Without wanting to offer God our thanks?

How can we see the seasons come and go
In an orderly pattern
And not trust God with our lives?

How can we see how unique a creation
Each and every person is
And not appreciate each as one of God's precious gifts?

As it says in the Bible,
"O, taste and see that the LORD is good."

Enjoy the varied experiences of life
And live with a grateful heart.

Karyl J. Leslie

It Hurts to Keep It Inside

God.
I feel your love.
I see your love
for all you have created,
are creating,
will create.
I feel it differently than I have.
It does not bring bubbling joy –
this time.
It brings a yearning,
a deep longing,
a hungering.
Not for something *for* me,
But for something *from* me.
It hurts to keep it inside.

God.
I need to share your love.
I need to show your love.
I need to be your love
to somebody,
in someone's life.
But to whom,
in whose life?
It is wonderful.
But
it hurts to keep it inside.

God.
Provide me with someone
who needs your love.
Show me someone
with whom I can share your love.
Give me someone
to whom I can be your love.

You know
it hurts to keep it inside.

God.
Your love was not given to be mine,
to be his,
to be hers,
to be any one's,
But to be *ours*,
together...
together...
together...
It is given for all of us,
it is given through all of us,
it is given to be in all of us.
It is given to be ours –
together...
Together with each other,
together with you,
together with all of your creation.

And God,
That is why
it hurts so much
to keep it inside.

KARYL J. LESLIE

A Song of Gladness

It's time to try to write a poem,
So that's what I will do.
It may be short, it may be long.
It may, indeed, become a song,

A song of gladness and of hope
In God, whose great love helps me cope
With life as it comes on each day.
That you might know this, too, I pray.

Benediction

What can I say to bless you today?
What can I say to bless you?

"May God's face shine upon you," I say.
"May God's grace be real in your life."

KARYL J. LESLIE

I Need You, Lord

God, take my hand
And don't let go.
I need your help
To make me grow.
I need your touch;
I need your care,
Your love around me
Everywhere.

I need to feel
Your strength with mine,
Supporting me
So I can climb
From the depths of hurt
To the heights of my soul,
Loving you only,
And thus being whole.

I'm here again
Looking to see
How much I believe
In your love for me.

Trees

I think
that all of us
should be
ever mindful
of the tree.
Its branches strong
it reaches up
and lives
proclaiming
it is loved.
It lifts its arms
up
to the sky
reaching
reaching
And sometimes
it seems
it reaches
to the clouds
and to the heavens
and to the sun.
The warmth
and breezes
it takes in
And shows us
it will
always win.
Even when
its leaves
do fall,
It is a sign
unto us all
To still have hope
and love
and faith

And still
reach up
on every day
Because our God
is always there
Waiting
to answer
every prayer.
Sometimes
we droop
like trees
bowed down
all full
of snow,
But even then
we have to know
That God's love
for us
is always
near,
And God will
never
cease
to care.

Every Day Thanksgiving

In November each year
We join with great cheer
In a great Thanksgiving Day.

We remember our God
And the path that was trod
By those who set out in deep faith.

We give thanks for our food,
We give thanks for what's good.
We eat 'til our bellies are full.

With families and friends,
We address God again
With thanks and with praise in our hearts.

But what is there here
That can't be held dear
On any other day of the year?

Aren't there things for thanks
In every day's banks
Of the riches God offers to us?

Blessings and graces
Fill all of the spaces
We leave in our lives for our God.

So give thanks every day.
Remember and pray,
And acknowledge the graces of God.

Karyl J. Leslie

Let Us Thank Our God Above

There is something truly beautiful about life:
Life that is lived,
Life that is felt,
Life that is experienced with somebody else.

There is a special beauty to living:
Living in hope,
Living in love,
Living in faith with your God above.

There is a wonderful warmth that always comes:
Comes to the heart,
Comes to the mind,
Comes to the spirit through all that you find.

There is a feeling you get which cannot be compared:
Compared to success,
Compared to wealth,
Compared to a mere state of physical health.

Life and love must go hand in hand;
A wonderful feeling spreads through the land.
Beautifully warm is a life that is lived;
Love of life is such a wonderful gift.

Living and loving are one and the same;
Neither should ever be played as a game.
Living is giving, and giving is loving:
Therefore conclude that living is loving.

"We love, because God first loved us."
Recognize this love we must
If we're to live life as we should.
God's love for us is eternally good.

God's love is now; it forever shall be.
From our sins God sets us free.
Life is promised through God's love –
Let us thank our God above!

God gave us others so we could feel
God's love for us as something real.
God through people shows this love –
Let us thank our God above!

God's love for us is ever here;
God's Presence is forever near.
Knowing this our spirits are healed;
Then we wish God's will revealed.

To do God's will is all we ask,
But sometimes it seems an impossible task.
Though we fail; yet does God love –
Let us thank our God above!

Let us thank our God above;
Thank God for such bounteous love,
Thank God for people whom we love –
Let us thank our God above!

Let us thank our God above;
Thank God for such never-ending love,
Thank God for life – lived through love –
Let us thank our God above!

Karyl J. Leslie

Evening Song

The day has come; the day has gone.
Let me end it with this song:
Glory to our God above
For showing us the greatest love,
Such great love we could not tell
That we could ever be loved so well.
That we are is clearly said
When the Bible's clearly read.

December Readings

Advent Blessings

Advent is a season,
A wonderful season each year,
When we prepare for Jesus
To come ever more near.
The prophets have foretold it.
Their message is quite clear:
God comes to us as Savior
So we don't have to fear.

The first Sunday each Advent
We light the candle of hope.
We let God reassure us,
So we don't have to mope.
The hope we have in Jesus
Can help us all to cope
With things that might dismay us
If we didn't have that hope.

The second Sunday of Advent,
We light the candle of peace,
For we believe that Jesus
Grants us a sweet release
From all the evils of Satan
Whose power will certainly cease
To threaten or undo us.
Thus we can live in peace:

Peace within our own hearts,
Peace in the world around,
Peace that touches our spirits
Whenever Christ's love abounds.
We can know that peace forever
If salvation we've found.
We don't have to fear the evils
That seem often to surround.

The third Sunday of Advent
We focus on holy joy.
We find our joy in Jesus
Beyond any kind of toy.
The candle of that Sunday
Is rose-colored through and through.
It celebrates the brightness
God gives to me and you.

Love is the crowning glory
Of the Advent candles; thus
It is the fourth Sunday's candle,
Reminding all of us
That God came in Christ for a reason
To add a great big plus
And show us love's the true way
To get through all that fuss.

On Christmas Eve or Morning,
We light the Christ candle, too,
To celebrate the good news
That Christ came for me and you.
He gives us light abundant.
He shines upon our way.
He came especially to give us
A new life every day.

Preparing the Way

A VOICE CRIES:
"IN THE WILDERNESS
PREPARE THE WAY OF THE LORD,
MAKE STRAIGHT IN THE DESERT
A HIGHWAY FOR OUR GOD."
(Isaiah 40:3)

"IN THE WILDERNESS..."
In what wilderness?
In the wilderness of the land?
of the societies?
of your own busy life?
of your own self/soul/spirit?

"...PREPARE THE WAY..."
How? What way?

"...THE WAY OF THE LORD..."
But what is the way of the Lord?
And how can we prepare it?

"MAKE STRAIGHT IN THE DESERT
A HIGHWAY FOR OUR GOD."

A highway is used for getting from one place to another.

This highway is "for our God."
Where is God coming from?
Where is God going to?

God comes from holiness, from love
to/into the heart of those God loves – all of us.

God comes to, but wants to come *into* the hearts, the lives, the souls
of God's people – *all* people.

This is the highway we are to prepare and make straight:
the highway *into* rather than just *to*.

We must clear out the paths for God's coming
to and into us.

We must expect God and be joyous in the expectation
and knowledge of God's coming –
to/into the land,
to/into the societies,
to/into our own busy lives,
to/into our own selves/souls/spirits.

Secrets

Do you ever have a secret
That you just can't wait to share?
Do you ever feel a joy inside
That you cannot keep in there?

Do you sometimes wish to shout aloud
From every mountaintop,
And tell to all the world around
The wonders God has brought?

It's a wonder and a pity
We just can't get to some,
Even when we try to tell them
What great things God has done.

The birth of Christ is one thing
We must try never to forget,
And to those who do not know Him
We must tell it even yet.

It's hard sometimes to realize
That God won't let us own,
But everywhere that we can go
God's love always abounds.

And so we have a secret
That we just can't wait to share,
And we each can feel a joy inside
That we cannot keep in there.

We must try always to shout aloud
From every mountaintop
And tell to all the world around
What wonders God has wrought.

"In the Beginning Was the Word"

"In the beginning was the Word."
It was very plainly heard
By those who had a listening ear
To hear what God's own angels hear.

The Word arrived with heavenly grace
To bring to every weary face
A smile that was so broad and wide
That nothing could that smile hide.

Have you yet received the touch
Of God, who loves us each so much
That God came to us in human form
To make our hopes grow very warm?

God has for each of us a plan
That no woman and no man
Can thwart and turn aside, you see.
God wants hope to rise for you and me.

But beware of Satan's schemes,
And even though sometimes it seems
That Satan has the winning hand,
That is not the thing God planned.

For good with God will triumph o'er
Any knock upon the door
That would bring sin to your heart.
God says instead, "Begone! Depart

From this one I claim with love,
A love that endures far above
Any sin that can deface
Or make this one feel all debased."

For forgiveness is the way
God lives with us on every day.
It's time to let God's love come in
And free your heart from every sin.

"In the beginning was the Word."
In Christ God came here to the earth
In a way no one would have guessed.
Now in this grace let your heart rest.

Karyl J. Leslie

Christmas Again

It's Christmas time.
It comes again,
As every year,
What happens then?

Some souls are troubled.
They don't find rest.
The birth of Christ
They don't confess.

They do not know
The meaning of
This time of year,
God's gift of love.

To them I say,
I understand.
Commercialism
Lies close at hand.

The gifts we buy,
The gifts we give:
Do they really
Help us live?

Throughout the year
We must admit
We remember not
God's holy gift.

What good is it
To spend so much
On many things
Yet not to touch?

The human heart
Needs to reach out;
Hands need to touch,
Love needs to shout.

Is it an act?
Do we really care?
What parts of us
Do we really share?

Is it a painting?
Is it a verse?
What is there in us
We need not rehearse?

What spontaneous
Gift can we give
As each day all year
Together we live?

God gave us a gift,
Sent love, God's own Son.
Each day God gives
And never is done.

What lesson can we
Learn in this year;
What gifts of love
Give to those we hold dear?

Love is the most
Important of all.
How do we show it
When others call?

Loneliness
Is hard to bear
Especially now
At this time of year.

Can we be sensitive?
Can we reach out
To others who need us
And feel so much doubt?

We must feel God's love
For us deep inside,
And must give it away
And not try to hide.

God gave us the Son,
Whose love ever stays.
Let's follow this One,
Who's showing the way.

A Christmas Blessing

May Christmas be for you this year
a time of holy mystery and blessing;
and may the New Year
bring you grace, peace, and joy untold.

Karyl J. Leslie

Christmas Eve

Dear God,
Here it's Christmas Eve again.
We've gathered 'round your throne.
On this most holy night of nights,
We know we're not alone.
For you have come to earth in Christ
To set your people free
From fear and shame and guilt and death,
From terrors there might be.
You've come to earth in human flesh,
A little baby new.
You've come to earth to be with us
And our whole world renew.
There is no wonder greater than
The words that are so true,
That you have come to earth as man.
What better could you do?
For you have come to show us how
Your love for us is great.
You have come to show us now
That love's stronger than hate.
We may be here with family,
We may have come alone,
But with each other we are blessed,
And this is our true home.
Here in your holy worship house
We gather once again
To bring the worship you are due
And all our lives amend.
We've come to know the peace you've brought,
A peace that can't be known
In any other way than that
We've mercy from your throne.
O God, this is the night of nights,
The holiest, the best,

And we have come and gathered here
To celebrate how blessed
Each and every one of us
Has been through Christ's shed blood;
And we pray that you will lift
Every sinking mood.
Whether it's grief with which we're pressed
In this beloved season,
Whether it's anger or dismay,
You love is the real reason
That we can have a hope each day
That life can better be;
Even as we gather round
A lovely Christmas tree.
The very branches of the tree
Are always green we know;
And that is to remind us
How your love just grows and grows
For each of us on every day.
Your love, it circles round;
And in a holy company
We sing a joyful sound.
Hope and peace and joy and love
Are represented here
By the Advent candles that
We light from year to year.
You are our fulfillment true,
Fulfillment of each dream
That is worthy of your grace
And not simply a scheme
To get us right in sight of man,
To make us look the part
Of the perfect-natured one.
Let's not even start
To portray ourselves as whole,
As good and kind and true,
When we each know our own selves

And the unkind things we do.
We gossip, lie, and sin and cheat,
Though we don't like to know
Even what is in our hearts.
It's easier, you know,
To blame our ills on someone else,
To let them hold the bag,
To say they are unworthy,
But on ourselves to brag.
This, O God, is holy time.
We've gathered in your name;
And we pray upon this night
We'll never be the same.
Come into our hearts as once
You came in manger rude.
Help us look to you and seek
The best spiritual food.
May each of us hence do your will
Gladly and with prayer.
And may we each with someone else
The greatest of news share:
That you, O God, the holy one,
The blessed Lord most dear,
Have come to us at Christmas time,
And now you're always near,
As near as is our very breath,
And the heart that beats
Within our chest in rhythm
That jumps with joy and greets
The great glad news of Christmas time
With hearts we open wide.
And let us find our peace in you
And walk with cheerful stride
As we seek to do your will
And love our neighbors, though

We may not always like them,
But it is enough to know
That you have loved us, every one,
And came in Christ to dwell
Within, beside, and around us
So we can always tell
That you are present in our lives.
You never will let go.
For you have come in Jesus Christ,
Your great love to bestow
On us mere mortal beings here
On the earth so round.
May we in your own presence blessed
Seek always to be found.
And so, O God, it's Christmas Eve,
A magic, special time,
And we have come to celebrate
Your majesty sublime,
Which you humbled to take part
In earthly life, as we
Come tonight to gather round
And know ourselves to be
Touched by the greatest love there is,
A love that came to dwell
Among us all at Bethlehem
And saved our souls from hell.
O God, you great and awesome one,
Your great glad news we know.
Help us, each one, to celebrate
Even as we go.
Amen, Amen, a great Amen,
May it truly be so
That we on each and every day
Your light in our lives show.

Karyl J. Leslie

My Christmas Prayer for You

May Christmas dawn upon you
So bright and full of joy
That you are as excited
As the most pleased girl or boy,

For you've received the present
You've wanted most of all,
The great big giant love of God
To be there when you call.

For God has answered even
Our most unconscious prayer,
The prayer we would be praying
If we knew how much God cared.

May Christmas shine upon you
With the remembrance strong
That in Christ God came to live with us
And save from sin and wrong.

Sparkling, Holy Light

May your holidays be bright
With God's creative light,
That brought the earth new hope,
Exceeding the wide scope
Of the people's hopes and fears
That they'd gathered through the years,
As on earth the Christ Child came,
Immanuel his name,
For he was God-made-flesh
And he showed us all the best
Of what God has in store
For those who hope for more:
More than the world's lame dreams,
More than the world's dumb schemes.
We now follow where Christ goes
And give thanks for what he shows.

Karyl J. Leslie

Immanuel – God Is With Us

The wise men knew,
The shepherds, too,
That this was someone special,

One who would grow
God's love to show
In life and death and all ways.

Mary conceived,
Joseph believed,
Hearing angels' words with trembling.

The Christ was born
That Christmas morn
And we today remember.

We celebrate,
Our souls elate:
God came to dwell among us!

So let us sing,
Let voices ring
With glad news one and all.

Our heart's voice raise
In ceaseless praise
For God's gift to us in Jesus.

Let's live our lives
That hope arise
Throughout the whole creation!

Let's dedicate,
Let's congregate.
Let's sing and praise and worship!

Then, days to come,
God's will be done
Through our lives led by Jesus.

Let's sing and pray,
Cast cares away,
For God is with us – holy!

Karyl J. Leslie

New Year's Eve

May Christ's light shine
in whatever darkness may try to overwhelm you;
may God's rich, deep, and amazing blessings
be with you now and forevermore;
and may you know much happy laughter
in the year to come.

Edwards Brothers Malloy
Thorofare, NJ USA
October 30, 2014